Visual Reference

CW00370058

Microsoft
PhotoDraw™ 2000

At a Glance

Stephen W. Sagman

Microsoft Press

PUBLISHED BY
Microsoft Press
A Division of Microsoft Corporation
One Microsoft Way
Redmond, Washington 98052-6399

Library of Congress Cataloging-in-Publication Data
Sagman, Stephen W.
    Microsoft PhotoDraw 2000 At a Glance / Stephen W. Sagman
       p.   cm.
    Includes index.
    ISBN 1-57231-954-2
    1. Computer graphics.   2. Microsoft PhotoDraw.   I. Title.
  T385.S2353 1999
  006.6ʹ869--dc21   98-31460
                                           CIP

Printed and bound in the United States of America.

1 2 3 4 5 6 7 8 9 QEQE 4 3 2 1 0 9

Distributed in Canada by ITP Nelson, a division of Thomson Canada Limited. A CIP catalogue record for this book is
available from the British Library.

Microsoft Press books are available through booksellers and distributors worldwide. For further information about
international editions, contact your local Microsoft Corporation office, or contact Microsoft Press International directly
at fax (425) 936-7329. Visit our Web site at mspress.microsoft.com.

Acquisitions Editor: Kim Fryer; Susanne Forderer
Project Editor: Jenny Moss Benson
Technical Editor: David Sagman

Contents

"How can I get started quickly in PhotoDraw?"

See page 6

Manage the
PhotoDraw window.
See page 17

"How do I scan a photo into PhotoDraw?"

See page 29

Get clip art.
See page 33

Create designer text.
See page 56

Crop an object.
See page 74

"How can I adjust the color in my photos?"

See page 95

"How do I repair a damaged photo?"

See page 104

Put a photo on a 3-D object.
See page 123

"How do I reuse images in other pictures?"

See page 137

Draw shapes.
See pages 154–64

"How do I adjust a shape I've created?"

See page 170

Acknowledgments

I'd like to thank my friends at Microsoft Press, including Kim Fryer, Susanne Forderer, Casey Doyle, and Lucinda Rowley, for giving me the opportunity to spend a few months with such a fun product. Jenny Moss Benson deserves a medal for her care, not to mention endurance, as my editor.

On the Studioserv team, Sharon Bell, of Presentation Desktop Publications, toiled relentlessly and with astounding precision and professionalism on revision after revision of the pages from her office on Vancouver Island. Thank you, Sharon!

Also on the Studioserv team, David Sagman, my father, graciously accepted the role of PhotoDraw neophyte, testing this book as part of his emerging, post-retirement status as physician-turned-computer geek. He reports that he tried the procedures and the right things happened each time. Thank you, dad!

Finally, of course, thank you patient Eric and my little love Lola.

About This Book

Microsoft PhotoDraw 2000 At a Glance is for anyone who wants to get the most from Microsoft Photo-Draw with the least amount of time and effort. I think you'll find this book to be a straightforward, easy-to-read, and easy-to-use reference tool. With the premise that your computer should work for you, not the other way around, this book's purpose is to help you get tasks accomplished quickly and efficiently so that you can take advantage of PhotoDraw and use it to the max.

No Computerese!

Let's face it—when you don't know how to do a task but you need it done in a hurry, or when you're stuck in the middle of a task and can't figure out what's next, there's nothing more frustrating than reading page after page of technical background information. You want to know how to get it done—nothing more, nothing less—and you want it now! And the information should be easy to find and understand.

That's what this book is all about. It's written in plain English—no technical jargon and no computerese. No single task in the book takes more than two pages. Just look up what you need to know about in the index or the table of contents, turn to the page, and there it is. Each introduction to a task gives you information that is essential to carrying out the task, suggests situations in which you can use the task, or provides examples of the benefit you gain from performing the task. The task itself is laid out step by step and accompanied by graphics that add visual clarity. Just read the introduction, follow the steps, look at the illustrations, and get your work done with a minimum of hassle.

You may want to turn to another task if the one you're working on has a "See Also" in the left column. Because there's a lot of overlap among tasks, I wanted to bring you through the tasks in such a way that they would make sense to you. I've also added some useful tips here and there and offered a "Try This" once in a while to give you a context in which to use the task. But, by and large, I've tried to remain true to the heart and soul of the book, which is that information you need should be available to you at a glance.

Useful Tasks...
Whether you use PhotoDraw for work, play, or some of each, I've tried to pack this book with procedures for everything I could think of that you might want to do, from the simplest tasks to some of the more esoteric ones.

...And the Easiest Way to Do Them
Another thing I've tried to do in *Microsoft PhotoDraw 2000 At a Glance* is to tell you the easiest way to accomplish a task. PhotoDraw often provides many ways to accomplish a single result, which can be daunting or delightful, depending on the way you like to work. If you like to stick with one favorite and familiar approach, I think the methods described in this book are the way to go. If you prefer to try out alternative techniques, go ahead! The intuitiveness of PhotoDraw invites exploration, and you're likely to discover ways of doing things that you think are easier or that you like better. If you do, that's great! It's exactly what the creators of PhotoDraw had in mind when they provided so many alternatives.

A Quick Overview
You don't have to read this book in any particular order. The book is designed to be kept near your computer so that you can jump in, pick up the information you need, and then turn back to work. But that doesn't mean I scattered the information about with wild abandon. If you were to read the book from front to back, you'd find a logical progression from basic tasks to more sophisticated procedures. Here's a quick overview.

First, I assume that PhotoDraw is already installed on your computer. If it's not, the Setup program makes installation so simple that you won't need my help anyway. So, unlike most computer books, this one doesn't start out with installation instructions and a list of system requirements. You've already got that under control.

Sections 2 and 3 of the book cover the basics: starting PhotoDraw, using the Microsoft PhotoDraw dialog box when you start PhotoDraw, understanding the parts of the PhotoDraw screen, and managing the PhotoDraw window so you can get the best view of your work.

Sections 4 and 5 describe the sources for images that you can work with: scanners that you use to convert real photos to PhotoDraw pictures, digital cameras from which you can download pictures right into PhotoDraw, and the Clip Gallery, where you will find a huge library of ready-made graphics for your projects.

Section 6 covers the basics of adding text to your pictures and using the many techniques that you can use to convert plain text into extraordinary graphics.

Section 7 describes the ways that you can manipulate individual objects in PhotoDraw pictures: flipping them, skewing them, cropping them, erasing parts of them, and much more.

Section 8 explores the commands you can use in PhotoDraw to modify and enhance the color in the images you've created or the photos you've scanned or downloaded.

Section 9 takes a look at the tools that PhotoDraw offers for retouching and repairing photos so you can transform every snapshot you've taken to photographic perfection.

Section 10 describes the multitude of effects that you can apply to any image to turn ordinary photos into anything from fun and playful images to museum-quality works of art.

Section 11 reveals the ways that you can combine images and even bits and pieces of images into complete compositions, mixing and matching items from other PhotoDraw pictures.

Section 12 shows you how to start projects by using the dozens of ready-made designs provided in templates. When you personalize these generic templates, you can create graphics that look professionally tailored for your needs.

Sections 13 and 14 cover drawing and painting in PhotoDraw. They describe how to draw objects, paint pictures, and modify the shapes of the drawings you've made.

Section 15 describes the steps you take only after you've put the finishing touches on a picture: saving it in a file, saving it in a format that's suitable for use in another program or on a Web page, sending it by e-mail, or printing it out so you can have a copy on paper.

Section 16 is unlike other sections in the book because it takes you through a short project that shows how you might integrate a number of PhotoDraw's capabilities to obtain something useful; in this case, a set of matching buttons for a Web page.

Section 17 wraps up by showing you how to get assistance as you work in PhotoDraw, both by using the Help system that's built into the program and by visiting the PhotoDraw Assistance Web page on the Internet, where you can not only ask questions and review the most common questions and answers from other people, but also download updates to the program and enhancements, such as new templates.

A Final Word (or Two)

I had three goals in writing this book. I want the book to help you:

◆ Do all the things you want to do with PhotoDraw.

◆ Discover how to do things you didn't know you could do with PhotoDraw.

◆ Enjoy using PhotoDraw.

My "thank you" for buying this book is the achievement of those goals. I hope you'll have as much fun using *Microsoft PhotoDraw 2000 At a Glance* as I've had writing it. The best way to learn is by doing, and that's what I hope you'll get from this book.

Jump right in!

2

Getting Started

A blank canvas: it's what you face in most art programs. But Microsoft PhotoDraw won't intimidate you that way. It lets you start with something—an image you've scanned, a photo you've taken with a digital camera, or a file on a disk—and then work on it. Or, it lets you start with a design template whose generic text and photos you replace with your own.

Of course, you can start with a blank picture, too, adding new text and graphic elements or borrowing them from other pictures. In fact, PhotoDraw was developed to make it easy to reuse bits and pieces of existing pictures in your new compositions.

If you've got the artistic talent, you can draw and paint all the bits and pieces you need. But if you're like most people, you'll use the giant clip art collection and thousands of photos that come with PhotoDraw. Or, if you have a scanner or digital camera, you can use your own pictures and recombine them, frame them, or apply special effects that make them look like anything from an impressionist watercolor to a post-modern art piece.

It all begins when you start PhotoDraw. And fortunately, PhotoDraw starts by giving you some simple choices.

Starting PhotoDraw

PhotoDraw does something special each time it starts: it welcomes you with the Microsoft PhotoDraw dialog box, which opens right in the middle of the PhotoDraw window.

The Microsoft PhotoDraw dialog box offers a menu of the tasks that you are most likely to start with, such as opening a new, blank picture, scanning a new photo, or opening a picture that you have worked on recently.

TIP

Disabling the Microsoft PhotoDraw dialog box.
If you'd rather use PhotoDraw's menus and toolbars to accomplish opening tasks, you can turn off the Microsoft Photo-Draw dialog box by clicking the "Don't Show This Dialog Box Again" check box in the dialog box.

Start PhotoDraw

1 Click the Start button on the Windows taskbar.

2 Point to Programs.

3 Click Microsoft PhotoDraw on the Programs menu.

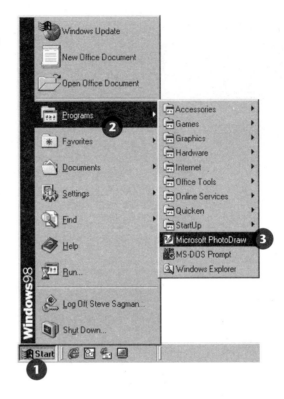

The Microsoft PhotoDraw Dialog Box

The Microsoft PhotoDraw dialog box is a great help when you are new to PhotoDraw because it gets you up and running with a clear list of common first steps. You'll probably still want to use the Microsoft PhotoDraw dialog box when you're a veteran PhotoDraw user because it gives you one-click access to the most common starting tasks.

But before you get too hooked on the dialog box, remember that it appears only when you first start Photo-Draw. To get back to it when you're ready to start something new, you have to quit and then restart PhotoDraw between projects, and that's not always possible. There may be times, for example, when you want to scan a new photo for a picture you are currently working on.

Fortunately, each task in the Microsoft PhotoDraw dialog box has a matching button on one of the toolbars that is visible in the PhotoDraw window. The toolbar buttons let you accomplish everything you can do by clicking options in the Microsoft PhotoDraw dialog box. You don't have to leave the program and come back in to accomplish basic chores like starting a blank picture or downloading a photo from a digital camera. For example, to accomplish the first option on the Microsoft PhotoDraw dialog box, starting a new, blank picture, you can click the New button on the Standard toolbar.

This chapter covers the tasks that you can accomplish when you first start PhotoDraw and use the Microsoft PhotoDraw dialog box to get going. In later chapters, you learn to carry out the same tasks with toolbar buttons.

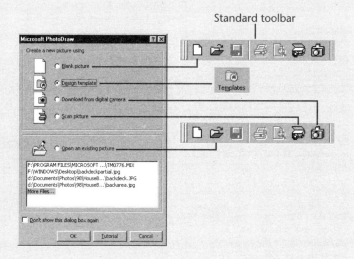

Standard toolbar

Starting Something New

When you start PhotoDraw, the Microsoft PhotoDraw dialog box gives you the choice to create a new picture or open an existing file.

If you want a new picture, you choose whether to use a design template, download a photo, or scan an image. If you'd rather start from scratch with a blank picture, you select its size (anything from a large, full-page picture to a small picture sized for a business card). Then you're off and running.

TIP

How and when the Microsoft PhotoDraw dialog box appears. *The Microsoft PhotoDraw dialog box described in these procedures appears only when you start PhotoDraw. If PhotoDraw is open when you want to start a new picture, you must click New on the File menu, instead.*

Start a New Picture When You Start PhotoDraw

1. Start PhotoDraw.

2. Click Blank Picture in the Microsoft PhotoDraw dialog box.

3. Click OK.

4. On the Pictures or Labels tab of the New dialog box, click your choice of picture size.

5. Click OK.

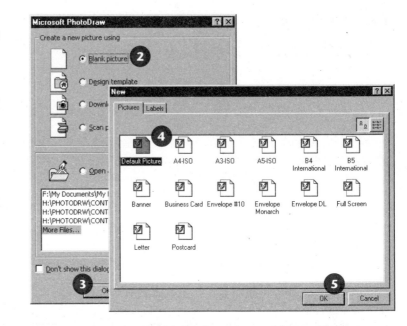

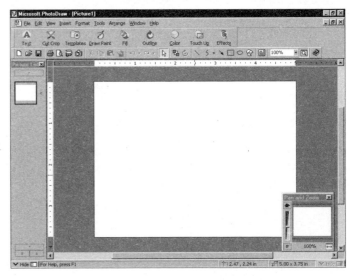

SEE ALSO

For more information on scanning and downloading images from digital cameras, see Section 4, "Using Scanners and Digital Cameras."

TIP

Scanner or digital camera must be installed. *Before you can follow this procedure, you must have a scanner or digital camera installed.*

Download a Digital Photo or Scan an Image When You Start PhotoDraw

1. Start PhotoDraw.

2. Click Download From Digital Camera or Scan Picture.

3. Click OK.

4. Use the options on the Digital Camera workpane or the Scan workpane to either download or scan a photo.

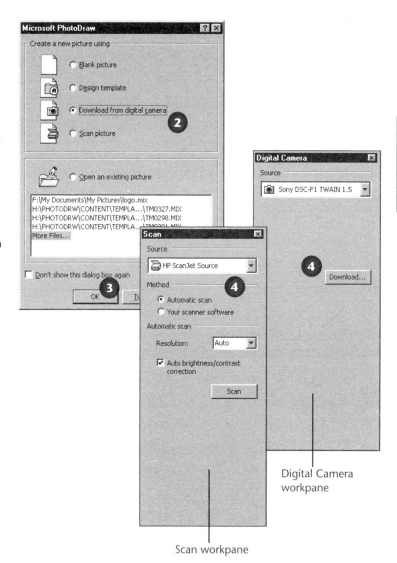

Digital Camera workpane

Scan workpane

The PhotoDraw Screen

At first glance, the PhotoDraw screen looks fairly complicated, but it helps to think of the screen as having five parts: the menu and toolbars at the top, the work area where you work on pictures in the middle, two panels left and right, and the status bar at the bottom. The left panel holds a list of the pictures you have open and the right panel, the workpane, holds the options for the tool you are currently using.

Menu and Toolbar Area

At the top of the PhotoDraw screen are the menu, the visual menu, and the toolbars. The menus (File, Edit, View, and so on) are standard Windows menus. You've seen a million of them. The *visual menu*, on the other hand, is unique. It has large buttons you can click to open menus of actions (the graphic sample next to each menu item shows the result of using the option). The Standard toolbar, just below the visual menu, contains buttons for the commands that you use most often.

You also may see a Formatting toolbar next to or below the Standard toolbar. This toolbar, which holds buttons for formatting text and graphic objects, is turned off by default. To turn on the Formatting toolbar, you can point to Toolbars on the View menu, and then click Formatting on the submenu.

The Work Area

At the center of the PhotoDraw screen is a large work area where you work on one or more pictures. The current picture is at the top of the stack of pictures that you have open and it fills this area. Although you see only the topmost picture at first, you can restore each picture in the work area so it has its own window and set of rulers. You can also minimize each picture so it becomes a button at the lower-left corner of the work area, or maximize a picture so it once again fills the work area.

The Picture List

The picture list has one entry (a thumbnail image) for each picture that you have open. By clicking a thumbnail on the picture list, you can move that picture to the front of the stack in the work area for editing.

The Workpane

The workpane opens to show the options for the tool you select. While you apply a shadow to an image, for example, the workpane displays a gallery of shadow directions along with options you can use to set the shadow transparency and softness.

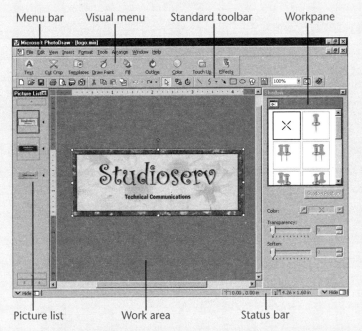

Menu bar   Visual menu   Standard toolbar   Workpane

Picture list   Work area   Status bar

A workpane appears when you select a tool or command that has options, and it overlaps the work area. It may overlap part of the picture you are working on. To fix this, press the F11 key to reduce the zoom level so the picture fits neatly in the work area. After you close the workpane, press the F11 key to zoom back in on the picture.

After you finish working with a tool, you can close the workpane by clicking the Close button at the upper right corner of the workpane. When the workpane closes, you gain more work area within the PhotoDraw window.

The Status Bar

The status bar, a thin horizontal strip along the bottom of the PhotoDraw window, tells you the position and size of the object you are working on, and it indicates with an undulating blue strip when the program is busy applying an effect or carrying out an action. The Hide buttons at the left and right ends of the status bar let you hide the picture list and workpane. The Hide buttons then become Show buttons that you can click to restore the picture list and workpane.

Opening Something Old

When you start PhotoDraw, you can choose to open an existing picture that you want to work on more. You can also open an existing picture when you are working in PhotoDraw to borrow something from it for another picture. Because you can open several pictures at once and reuse objects from various pictures, you can mix and match parts of pictures to form new images.

When you look for an existing picture, you can use *Visual Open*, which displays small versions of all the pictures in each folder. Visual Open lets you open a picture by sight rather than by the name of its file.

Start with a Picture You Worked on Recently When You Start PhotoDraw

1. Start PhotoDraw.

2. Click a picture listed by name in the Microsoft PhotoDraw dialog box.

3. Click OK.

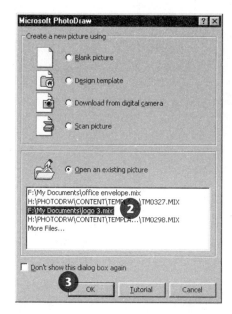

Open a Recent Picture When PhotoDraw Is Already Started

1. At the bottom of the File menu, click one of the recently opened pictures listed by name.

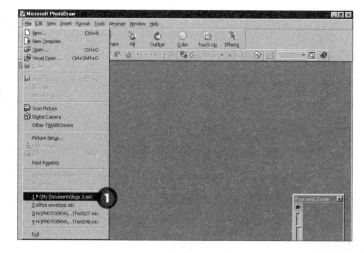

Filtering the file list. *You can type the first few letters of the file name in the File Name box and click Open to filter the pictures that are shown. Only pictures whose file names match the first few letters are shown.*

Browse for a Picture When You Start PhotoDraw

1. Click Visual Open on the File menu.

2. Click a disk and folder in the Look In list.

3. If you want, click the drop-down arrow next to the Files Of Type box and click a type of graphics file to display.

4. Click a preview.

5. Click Open to open that picture.

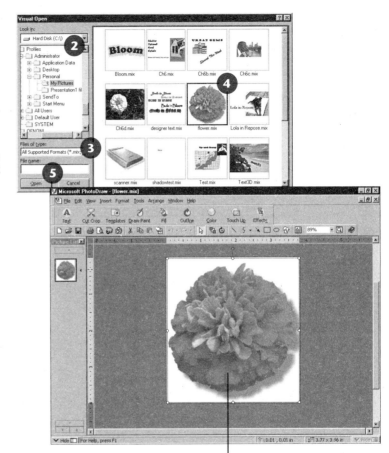

Opened picture

Inserting a Photo into a Picture

After you start a new picture and choose a size (whether you want to create a post-card, a Web page banner, or a CD insert), you can begin to insert objects into the picture. You can insert text and clip art, but you probably want to center a picture around a photo.

TIP

Previewing images. *To see a preview of each image you click on the Insert dialog box, click the Preview button on the toolbar in the dialog box.*

Insert a Photo from a File After You Have Opened a Blank Picture

1 Click From File on the Insert menu.

2 Click the drop-down arrow next to the Look In box, and click the folder that has the file.

3 Click a photo file.

4 Click Open.

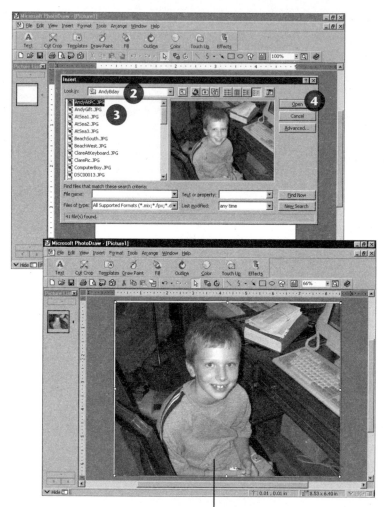

Inserted photo

Browsing for a Photo to Insert

Unlike the preview that you can view in the standard Insert dialog box, which shows the selected photo file, the PhotoDraw *Visual Insert* feature lets you see miniature, thumbnail versions of all the photos in a folder. Rather than try to remember a photo by file name, you can view the photos and select one by sight. Visual insert is similar to visual open.

TRY THIS

Royalty-free photos for your pictures. *Put the second PhotoDraw CD into your CD-ROM drive and click Photo-Draw Content on the Insert menu to browse the large selection of royalty-free photos you can insert into pictures.*

Visual Insert a Photo After You Have Opened a Blank Picture

1. Click Visual Insert on the Insert menu.

2. In the Look In list, click the disk and folder that has the file.

3. Click a preview.

4. Click Insert.

Inserted photo

About the Picture List

Although the visual menu is pretty unique, the *picture list* gives you the power to mix and match parts of PhotoDraw pictures to create new compositions.

Think of the picture list, at the left side of the PhotoDraw window, as a display of thumbnails of all the pictures you have open. The picture list can also list each item in every picture (each photo, shape, or text item). In PhotoDraw, the items in pictures are called *objects*. To see a list of the objects in a picture, click the small, right arrow button next to the picture. The objects appear on a pop-out list and they're in order from front in the picture to back. In other words, if the objects overlap in the picture, the object at the top of the overlap is at the top of the object list.

You can also think of the picture list as a filing cabinet for the pictures with which you are currently working. The thumbnails in the picture list, one for each open picture, are the drawers of the filing cabinet. When you open a drawer by clicking the right-arrow button, you can look inside and see all the objects in a particular picture.

As you will learn in Section 11, "Combining Images," you can drag an object from any picture's object list to the picture in the work area. This lets you copy parts of one picture into another, and compose new pictures that reuse parts of other pictures. You can take a logo that you created for the picture that shows your letterhead, and copy it into another picture for your company envelopes.

The picture list also lets you easily select one object in a picture that is composed of many objects. When you have selected the object you want, you can edit just that one part of the picture.

Picture list

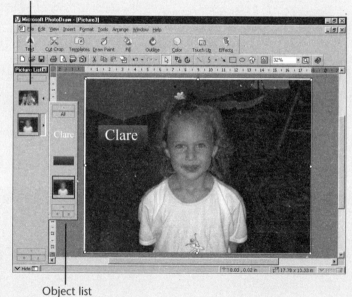

Object list

3

Managing the PhotoDraw Window

As you work in Microsoft PhotoDraw, you will sometimes find that you need to adjust the PhotoDraw window. Often, workpanes open and cover part of the picture. At other times, you need to move the view of your work a little to one side or the other to focus on a different subject or area within the picture.

These basic PhotoDraw tasks and others are the subject of this section, which covers both reorienting your view as you work and setting up the PhotoDraw window so it works in a way that is comfortable and productive for you.

Zooming the Screen

The Pan And Zoom dialog box makes it easy to zoom in to a spot on a picture and work with the detail.

TIP

Zooming in and out. *The Zoom drop-down list on the toolbar lets you choose a zoom level by percentage. It also gives you these convenient choices: Selection (zoom to fit the objects you've selected to the work area), Fit All (zoom to fit everything in the picture within the work area), or Fit Picture Area (zoom to fit the entire picture within the work area).*

TIP

Zooming out quickly. *To quickly zoom out to see everything in the entire picture, you can click the Fit To Picture Area button at the lower-right corner of the Pan And Zoom dialog box.*

Zoom In and Out

1 Click the Pan And Zoom button on the toolbar.

2 Drag the slider up or down or click the Zoom In or Zoom Out button above and below the slider in the Pan And Zoom dialog box.

Before zoom   After zoom   Pan And Zoom button

Pan And Zoom dialog box

Panning Across the Screen

After you zoom in, you can pan across the screen to the left, right, up, or down, and then work at a different spot on a picture. Panning allows you to drag the zoomed in view of a picture and center a different part of it within the work area.

TIP

Keeping the Pan And Zoom dialog box available. *You can leave the Pan And Zoom dialog box open at one corner of the screen so it is always readily available.*

SEE ALSO

For more information about zooming, see "Zooming the Screen" on page 18.

Pan Across the Screen

1. Click the Pan And Zoom button on the toolbar.

2. Drag the slider up in the Pan And Zoom dialog box to zoom in to the picture.

3. Drag the red rectangle in the Pan And Zoom dialog box to a new position on the thumbnail. The picture is panned to the new position.

Before pan to the left   After pan to the left   Pan And Zoom button

Fitting the Picture Area

PhotoDraw's Fit To Picture Area command instantly zooms in or out as required to fit the picture area neatly within the visible work area. Use it when you can't see the entire picture, either after you've zoomed in or after a workpane opens and covers part of the picture area.

The Fit To Picture Area command is also available by pressing the F11 key.

TIP

The Fit To Picture Area button. *The Fit To Picture Area command is also available in the Pan And Zoom dialog box.*

Fit to Picture Area

1 Click Fit To Picture Area on the View menu.

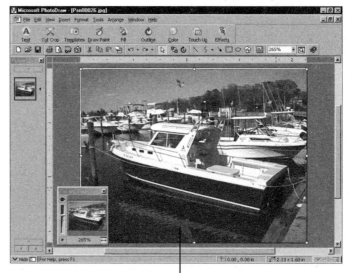

Picture area fits neatly within the work area.

Fitting All Objects on the Work Area

To see all objects in the work area, even those that are outside the white picture area, use the Fit To All command.

TIP

The scratch area. *The scratch area, the gray area surrounding the white picture area is a space upon which you can place objects to put them out of the way temporarily while you focus on objects in the picture area.*

Fit the View to See All Objects

1 Click Fit To All on the View menu.

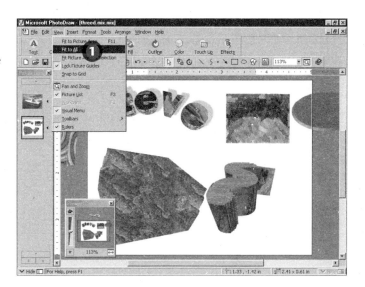

Objects on the scratch area

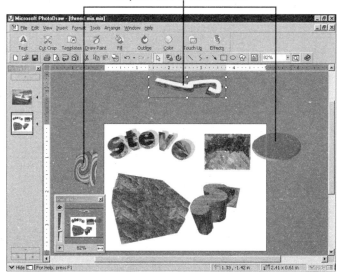

Fitting the Picture Area to Objects

If the object or the set of objects you are working on is larger or smaller than the picture area, you can use the Fit Picture Area To Selection command to resize the picture area so it fits the selected objects. When you save the contents of the picture area to a graphics file, the file will neatly contain the objects.

TIP
Selecting multiple objects.
To select more than one object, you can hold down the Shift key and click each object.

Fit the Picture Area to a Selection

1 Click an object or select more than one object in the work area.

2 Click Fit Picture Area To Selection on the View menu.

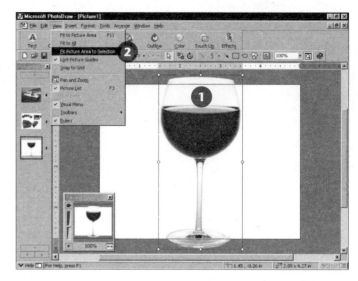

Picture area has been fitted to the selected object.

Setting Up the Picture Area

When you start PhotoDraw, or when you start a new picture, you can choose a picture size from a list of standard sizes.

If the size you want is not on the list, you can specify any custom size in inches, centimeters, millimeters, or pixels.

TIP

A dummy Web page. *If you are designing Web page graphics, you can set up the picture area so it's the size of a typical Web page. Change the units to pixels and use a size of approximately 600 pixels wide by 300 pixels high. This is roughly the size of the viewing area in a Web browser on a 640-by-480-pixel desktop size.*

Set Up the Picture

1. Click Picture Setup on the File menu.

2. Click the drop-down arrow next to the Units box and choose a unit of measurement.

3. Enter dimensions in the Width and Height boxes.

4. Click Portrait or Landscape to change the orientation of the picture area.

5. To change the color of the picture area, click the drop-down area next to the Color box and click a color in the list.

6. Click OK.

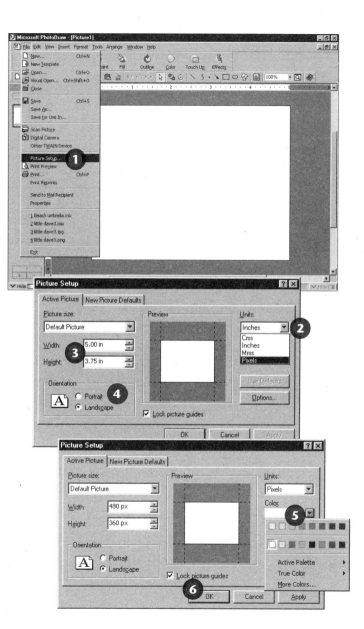

Setting the Default Size for New Pictures

Whenever you start a new picture by clicking the New Picture button on the Standard toolbar, PhotoDraw opens a new picture that is sized according to the new picture default settings.

You can change these settings to change the size of all new pictures.

TIP

When to change the default. *You may want to change the default size for new pictures if you usually create the same type of graphics, such as Web page elements.*

Set New Picture Defaults

1. Click Picture Setup on the File menu.

2. Click the New Picture Defaults tab.

3. Click the drop-down arrow next to the Units box and choose a unit of measurement.

4. Enter dimensions in the Width and Height boxes.

5. Click Portrait or Landscape to change the orientation of the picture area.

6. To change the color of the picture area, click the drop-down area next to the Color box and click a color in the list.

7. Click OK.

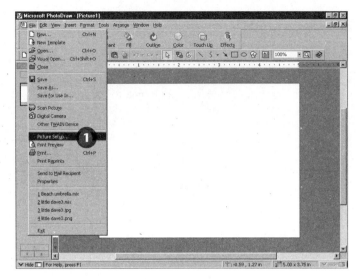

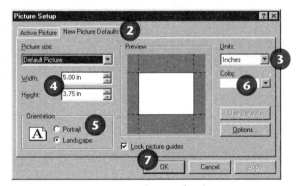

Resizing the Picture Area

The easiest way to resize the picture area is by dragging the picture guides with the mouse. When you unlock the picture guides, they become visible so you can drag them to change the size or shape of the picture area.

Drag the Picture Guides

1. Click Lock Picture Guides on the View menu to make the picture guides visible.

2. Drag one or more picture guides horizontally, vertically, or diagonally to resize the picture area.

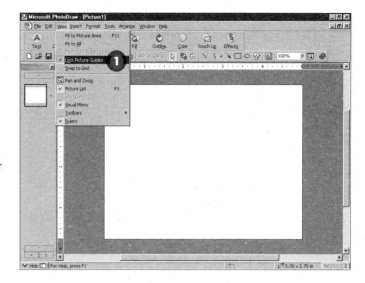

Picture guides

3

Setting Up the Grid

You can't see the grid, but you will notice objects jump to it as you drag them when Snap To Grid is turned on.

The grid helps you drag objects into precise positioning. As you drag objects, they jump from one grid point to the next, which keeps them neatly lined up.

Turn On Snap To Grid

1 Click Snap To Grid on the View menu.

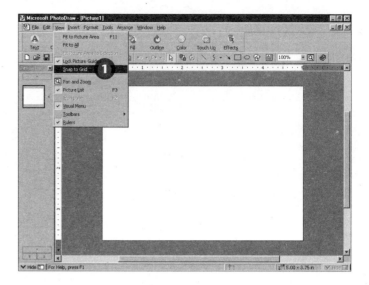

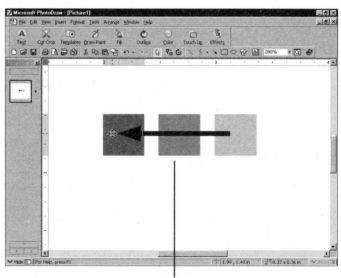

The object being moved snaps to half-inch increments when the grid spacing is set to 0.5 inches.

Using Scanners and Digital Cameras

Microsoft PhotoDraw can work wonders with clip art and photos that you download from the Internet, but if you want to work with your own photos, you need either a scanner or a digital camera. A scanner converts actual photos into computer pictures. After you place a photo on the glass plate of a scanner, PhotoDraw starts the scanner and reads the photo directly into a PhotoDraw picture. PhotoDraw can even straighten a crooked image and adjust its brightness and contrast before displaying it on the screen. If you have a digital camera, you can shoot your own photos and then have PhotoDraw download the photos directly into PhotoDraw pictures, too.

To communicate with scanners and digital cameras, PhotoDraw relies on special software, called TWAIN, which usually comes with these devices and is installed by their setup programs. If your scanner or digital camera did not come with TWAIN software, you must use the software that did come with your device to transfer photos into files on your hard disk drive. After the pictures you've scanned or photographed are in disk files, you can then insert them into PhotoDraw pictures.

Setting Up a Scanner

If you install a new scanner and then start a scan, Photo-Draw asks you to identify the type of the scanner. Your choices are *flatbed scanner*, which has a sheet of glass on-to which items to be scanned are placed, or an *other* scanner, which encompasses sheetfed scanners, into which you feed pages one at a time, and handheld scanners that you move across an image.

When you identify the scanner type, you can also choose a performance level, which determines the technical method the software uses to pass data from the scanner to the software. Enhanced is the best and fastest choice, but if you have trouble with your scanner, try the other option, Normal.

If you install a new digital camera and choose to download pictures, Photo-Draw also asks you to identify the camera using the same procedure.

Identify Your Scanner or Camera

1. Click Options on the Tools menu.

2. Click the Scanner/ Camera tab.

3. Click your scanner on the list.

4. Click the Modify button.

5. Click the device type that matches your device.

6. Leave the Performance set to Enhanced. You should change it to Normal only if you have trouble with your scanner or camera.

7. Click OK to close the Modify Device Type dialog box.

8. Click OK to close the Options dialog box.

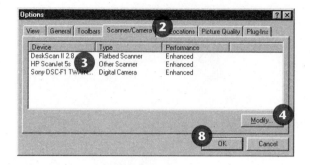

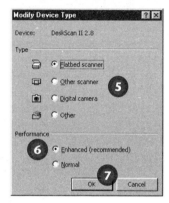

Starting an Automatic Scan

PhotoDraw's automatic scan is a remarkably powerful feature. It scans a preview of the image you have placed in the scanner, finds the area that contains the photo and crops away everything else, and automatically straightens an image that you put into the scanner crooked.

An automatic scan has two stages. First it scans a preview so it can find the image and straighten it. Then it performs the final scan. You can see these stages progress by watching the status bar at the bottom of the PhotoDraw window.

TIP

New images get new pictures. *PhotoDraw always scans an image into a new picture rather than inserting the image into the current picture. You can then drag the image into the current picture or another picture that is open.*

Scan a Picture

1. Click the Scan Picture button on the Standard toolbar.

2. Click a source in the Source drop-down list.

3. Leave Automatic Scan selected.

4. Leave the resolution at Auto to have Photo-Draw determine the best resolution for a photographic-quality image.

5. Clear the Auto Brightness/Contrast Correction check box only if you'd rather make these adjustments manually.

6. Click Scan. PhotoDraw scans your image into a new picture.

7. If you want, place another image on the scanner and click Scan again.

Scan Picture button

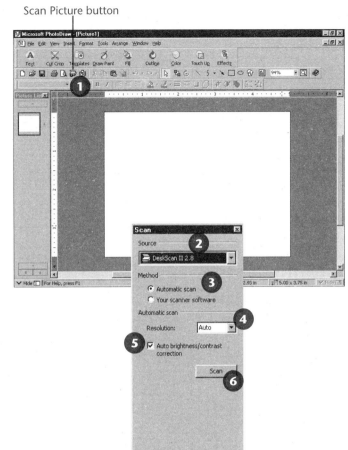

4

Choosing a Different Scanning Resolution

When you scan, PhotoDraw chooses a mid-level resolution of 150 dots per inch (dpi). This enables you to produce a photographic-quality print at an 8-by-10-inch print size. If you plan to use the image only on a Web page, you should choose a lower resolution, such as 96 DPI, the standard resolution of a monitor on which you view a Web page.

TIP

Start by scanning. *You can also choose to scan a picture in the Microsoft PhotoDraw dialog box, which appears each time you start PhotoDraw.*

Select a Resolution

1. Click the Scan Picture button on the Standard toolbar.

2. Click a numeric value in the Resolution drop-down list or type in an exact number, such as *96*.

3. Make other choices on the Scan workpane.

4. Click Scan.

Scan Picture button

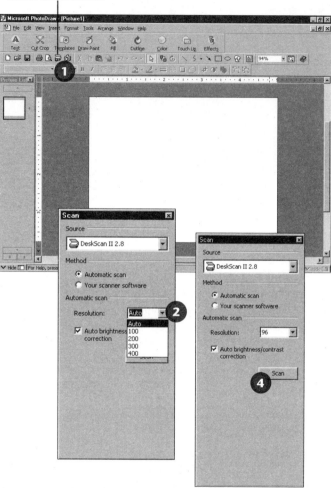

Using Your Scanner Software

You may want to use the scanning software that comes with your scanner to take advantage of features that are not available in Photo-Draw's automatic scan, such as automatic color correction or picture scaling. If you do, the automatic scan options, such as Resolution and Automatic Brightness/Contrast Correction, are grayed out.

The procedure on this page shows the scanning software for a Hewlett-Packard scanner. If you use a different model scanner, your scanning software dialog box will look different.

TIP

Automatic scan's special features. *Automatic picture straightening and automatic brightness and contrast correction are not available when you use your scanner's software rather than PhotoDraw's automatic scan.*

Use Your Scanner Software

1. Click the Scan Picture button on the Standard toolbar.

2. Click Your Scanner Software.

3. Click Scan. Your scanner software opens and displays its options in a dialog box.

4. Set the scanning options and start the scan using the options in your scanner software's dialog box.

Scan Picture button

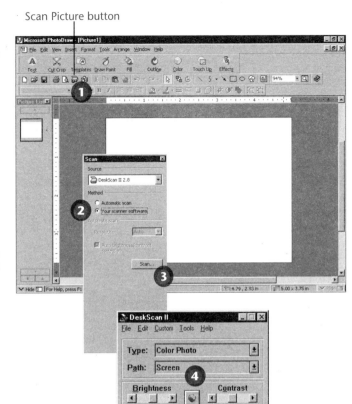

4

Downloading Photos from a Digital Camera

PhotoDraw can download photos from a digital camera. If the camera is a "Smart" model, its special software allows PhotoDraw to display thumbnails of the photos that are in the digital camera. If the digital camera is not a Smart camera (check the camera's documentation to determine whether it is), PhotoDraw starts the camera's software. You then use this software to choose and download images.

TIP

Digital photos are separate pictures. *Each photo that you download from a digital camera appears in a separate PhotoDraw picture. To insert a photo into the current picture, you can then drag it from the picture list.*

Download Photos

1. Click the Digital Camera button on the Standard toolbar.

2. Click your digital camera on the Source drop-down list.

3. Click Download.

   ◆ If your camera is a Smart camera, you can choose images to download by clicking thumbnails of the images that are in the camera.

   ◆ If your camera is not a Smart camera, or if you choose Custom Download, use the options in the digital camera software dialog box to select images and start the download.

Digital Camera button

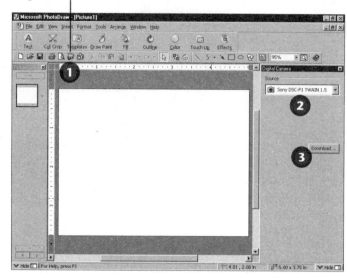

Digital camera dialog box for a Sony camera

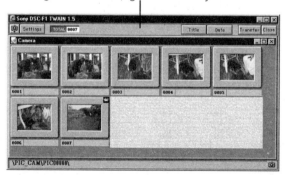

Getting Clip Art from the Clip Gallery

You may be familiar with clip art from using clip art libraries in other graphics programs. If so, you'll be surprised by the quality and variety of the more than 20,000 pieces of artwork in the Microsoft Clip Gallery.

The Clip Gallery works with Microsoft PhotoDraw to supply ready-made graphics for your pictures. It allows you to insert these images into your pictures and then use them as a basis for your own modifications. Using PhotoDraw's huge arsenal of special effects, you can transform a standard clip art image into something that's highly personal and truly unique.

Opening the Clip Gallery and Selecting a Category

Although the Clip Gallery looks like a part of Photo-Draw, it's really a separate program that you can use in any of the applications in Microsoft Office. Because the Clip Gallery opens in its own window, you can position it anywhere that's convenient, next to the PhotoDraw window or even partially overlapping it.

The clips in the Clip Gallery are organized into categories by subject. Be sure to scan through all the categories to find the one that is most relevant to your needs.

> **TIP**
>
> **Microsoft Office adds clip art.** *If you install Microsoft Office on your computer, the selection of clip art in the Clip Gallery may be greater.*

Open a Category in the Clip Gallery

1. Open the picture into which you want to insert clip art.

2. Click Clip Art on the Insert menu.

3. Insert the PhotoDraw CD that is requested.

4. Click a large category button. You can scroll down to see more category buttons.

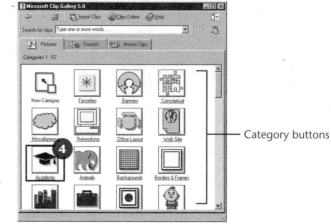

Category buttons

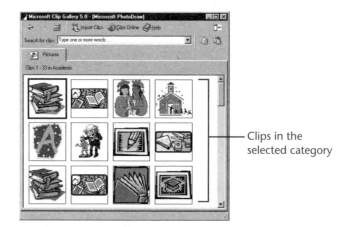

Clips in the selected category

Showing All Clip Categories

When you click a category button, the clips in that category appear in the Clip Gallery window as thumbnails. To see clips that are in a different category, you must get back to the display of all the category buttons.

SEE ALSO

To learn more about searching for clips, see "Searching for a Clip" on page 38.

TIP

Save screen space. *To shrink the Clip Gallery window so it occupies less screen space, click the Change To Small Window button near the upper-right corner of the Gallery window.*

Show All Categories

1 Click the All Categories button on the Clip Gallery toolbar. You can also press Alt+Home on the keyboard.

All Categories button

All categories become visible.

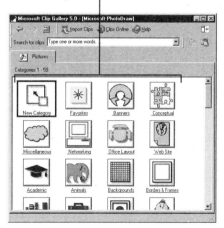

Inserting a Clip

When you find a clip that you want to place in a picture, you can insert it using the step-by-step instructions on this page. As you'll learn in the procedure on the opposite page, you can also drag a selection from the Clip Gallery window onto a picture in the PhotoDraw window, bypassing the Insert command altogether. Using the drag method allows you to insert multiple clips simultaneously.

Insert a Clip into the Current Picture

① Open the picture into which you want to insert clip art.

② Click Clip Art on the Insert menu to open the Clip Gallery.

③ Click a category in the Clip Gallery.

④ Click the thumbnail of the clip that you want to insert.

⑤ On the pop-out menu, click the Insert Clip button.

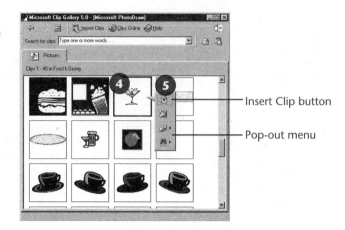

Insert Clip button

Pop-out menu

Dragging a Clip into a Picture

Rather than use the pop-out menu when you've found a relevant clip, you can simply drag a clip from the Clip Gallery window right onto a PhotoDraw picture. Dragging clips lets you insert multiple clips into a picture simultaneously. If you'd rather have the clip become its own picture on the picture list, you can drag the clip directly to the picture list, instead. Later, you can drag the clip from the picture list into a picture.

Drag a Clip into a Picture

1. Place the mouse pointer on a thumbnail in a category of the Clip Gallery or select multiple clips by holding down the Ctrl key as you click them.

2. Press and hold down the mouse button and drag the thumbnail or thumbnails into the current picture or onto the picture list.

3. Drag the clip from the upper-left corner of the work area, where PhotoDraw deposits it, into the proper position on the picture.

Dragging a picture

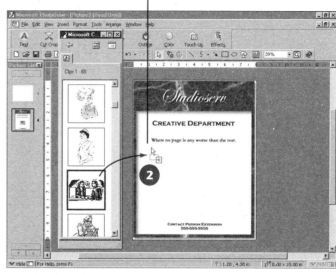

The clip after it is properly positioned on the picture

5

Searching for a Clip

Each clip in the Clip Gallery has a set of keywords that are relevant to the subject of the clip. To find appropriate clips in the gallery, you can enter search words that describe your need and let PhotoDraw match the keywords in the gallery. The Clip Gallery then shows thumbnails of clips that are relevant to your search.

The Clip Gallery is remarkably adept at matching concepts even if it finds no exact match to your search words. For example, entering *leadership* can find clips that have keywords like *executive* or *president*.

TIP

Editing clip keywords. *To view and edit the keywords attached to a clip, click the clip with the right mouse button. Choose Clip Properties from the shortcut menu, and then click the Keywords tab in the Clip Properties dialog box.*

Enter Search Words

1 Click Clip Art on the Insert menu to open the Clip Gallery.

2 Click in the Search For Clips box to select the text *Type one or more words.*

3 Type search words that are relevant to the subject of the clip you want. Separate the words with spaces.

4 Press Enter.

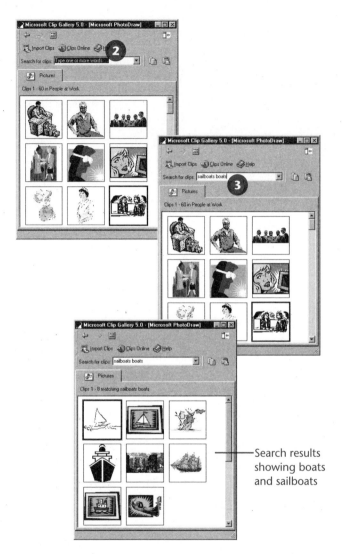

Search results showing boats and sailboats

Finding Similar Clips

After you open a category of clips, you may find a clip that is a good answer to your needs, but not perfect. By selecting the clip and then instructing the Clip Gallery to find similar clips, you may find an even more appropriate clip in a different category.

After you find a clip and then choose to find a similar clip, you can select one of the original clip's keywords to use as a search word, or even choose to find clips of the same artistic style or color and shape.

TIP

Assembling a montage.
Choosing to narrow the selection of clips to those of the same color and shape can help you maintain consistency when you are assembling elements for a montage.

Find a Similar Clip

1. Find a clip or choose a clip from a category.

2. Click the thumbnail for the clip.

3. On the pop-out menu, click the Find Similar Clips button.

4. Click a keyword on the Find Similar Clips panel or click the Artistic Style or Color & Shape buttons.

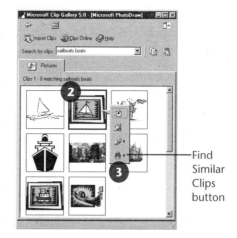

Find Similar Clips button

5

Previewing a Clip

The thumbnails you see in the Clip Gallery represent the actual images fairly well, but in some cases, large images have been shrunk down to small sizes to fit in the Clip Gallery window. To view an image at full size, you can preview it. The image opens full size in its own preview window.

> **TIP**
>
> **Clip Gallery doesn't show clip size.** *Some clips are quite small even though their thumbnails appear larger. These images have been stretched to fit the thumbnail squares. Don't be surprised if you preview a clip and find that it is actually a small icon in a tiny preview window.*

Preview a Clip

1. Click a thumbnail for a clip.

2. On the pop-out menu, click the Preview Clip button.

3. Click the Preview Clip button again to close the preview.

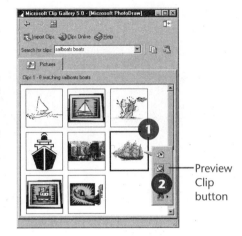

Preview Clip button

Preview window

Adding a New Category

If you've collected images for a project, you can store them in your own custom category in the Clip Gallery. You can create as many custom categories as you can invent original names, and each category can hold as many clips as you can store on your hard disk.

TIP

Use the Clip Gallery as a photo album. *Rather than buy photo album software that helps you store and catalog photos on your hard disk, you can use the Clip Gallery to keep photos that you've scanned or taken using a digital camera.*

TIP

The Clip Gallery category button image. *The button for the new category displays the first clip that you place in the new category.*

Add a Category

1 Click Clip Art on the Insert menu to open the Clip Gallery.

2 Click the New Category button.

3 Enter a name for the new category.

4 Click OK.

Cataloging Your Favorite Clips

If you find yourself using the same clips over and over, you can move them to the favorites category. The favorites category does not offer any special features, and it's no better than a custom category that you add and name yourself. It's just an easy place to collect clips that you use, because you can easily move clips to it.

> **TIP**
>
> **Copying clips between categories.** *You can also use this technique to copy a clip from one category into any other category.*

Move a Clip to the Favorites Category

1 Click Clip Art on the Insert menu to open the Clip Gallery.

2 Click a clip category and click a clip, or find a clip and then click it.

3 Click the Add Clip To Favorites Or Other Category button on the pop-out menu.

4 If you want to copy the clip to a category other than Favorites, select the category from the drop-down list.

5 Click Add.

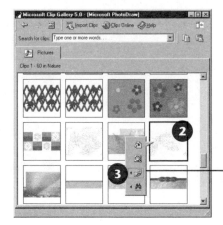

Add Clip To Favorites Or Other Category button

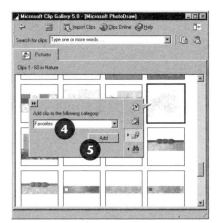

Shrinking the Clip Gallery Window

You can leave the Clip Gallery open while you work in PhotoDraw, but it occupies some space on the screen. To minimize the space used by the Clip Gallery, you can shrink the Clip Gallery window into a panel that is only wide enough to contain one column of category buttons or clips. If you want to browse in the Clip Gallery, you can always restore the window to its original size.

TIP

Minimizing the Clip Gallery. *You can also click the Minimize button at the upper-right corner of the Clip Gallery window to minimize the Clip Gallery to a button on the taskbar.*

Change to a Small Window

1. Open the Clip Gallery.

2. Click the Change To Small Window button.

Change To Small Window button

Shrunken Clip Gallery window

Click here to restore the window to full size.

5

Bringing Objects into the Clip Gallery

You can supplement the artwork in the Clip Gallery by importing image files. These image files may be collections of artwork that you have purchased from clip art companies, or they may be collections of pictures that you have downloaded from the Internet.

You can also use the Clip Gallery to store images that you've scanned or taken with a digital camera. To store your own images in the Clip Gallery, you must know the folder in which they are stored on your computer's hard disk drive.

Import a Clip

1. Open the Clip Gallery and click the Import Clips button.

2. Click the Look In drop-down arrow, and select the folder where the files are stored.

3. Click the file that you want to import.

   ◆ To import more than one more file, hold down the Ctrl key as you click them.

4. Choose one of the Clip Import options.

   ◆ The Copy Into Clip Gallery option copies the picture files into the Clip Gallery and leaves the originals as is.

   ◆ The Move Into Clip Gallery option copies the picture files into the Clip Gallery and deletes the originals.

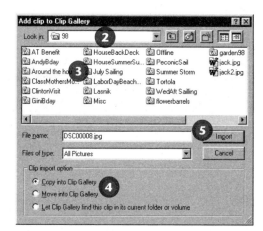

TIP

Save hard disk space.
When you install PhotoDraw, you can decide where the Clip Gallery catalogs will be stored on your hard disk, or whether they will be read from the CD-ROM drive. Leaving them on the CD saves hard disk space, but it's less convenient.

◆ The Let Clip Gallery Find This Clip In Its Current Folder Or Volume option does not copy the picture file into the Clip Gallery. Instead, it tells the Clip Gallery where to go to find the file on your hard disk drive or on your network.

⑤ Click Import.

⑥ Enter a description in the Description Of This Clip box.

⑦ Click the Categories tab and select categories in which the clip should appear.

⑧ Click the Keywords tab, click New Keyword for each new keyword you want to assign to the clip, and enter the keyword.

⑨ Click OK.

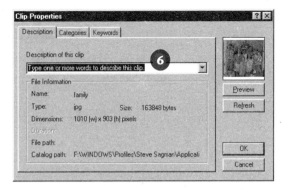

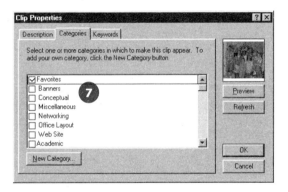

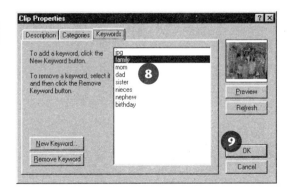

Downloading a Clip from Clip Gallery Live

As a free bonus to PhotoDraw users, Microsoft provides an area on its Web site, Microsoft Clip Gallery Live, from which you can download new clips for the Clip Gallery. These clips are free and you can use them in any project.

TIP

Special highlights in Clip Gallery Live. *Microsoft Clip Gallery Live frequently highlights special categories of clips, but you can also search through all the clips available at the Web site.*

Download a Clip from Clip Gallery Live

1 Connect to the Internet.

2 Open the Clip Gallery.

3 Click the Clips Online button.

4 Follow the instructions on the Clip Gallery Live Web page to download clips to the Clip Gallery.

Clips Online button

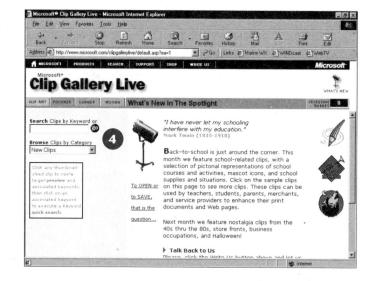

6

Adding Text

Although the primary emphasis in Microsoft Photo-Draw is working with photos, the program provides a surprisingly rich and full-featured set of tools for creating text effects. In fact, you may even be able to discard that special program you've been using to create 3-D text because PhotoDraw probably can do it just as well.

A text object in a PhotoDraw picture can be anything from a single character to a complete paragraph. It can be a simple label on a picture ("That's me on the right") or the main subject of a picture when you use PhotoDraw to fashion a text logo for a Web site or a business mailing.

In later sections, you learn to touch up and apply effects to photos. As you become familiar with these techniques, remember that they also can be applied to text objects. These effects, developed for photos but equally effective on text, give you enormous power to invent truly unique text stylings.

Inserting Text

You can add any number of text objects to a picture. Each text object appears as a separate item on the object list for the picture.

As you type text into the Text workpane, the characters appear on the picture. Their font, size, style, and color are determined by the options on the Text workpane. You can easily change these options before you begin typing or after you've entered the text you want.

> **TIP**
>
> **Entering text quickly.** *To quickly begin entering text, press Ctrl+T while you are working on a picture.*

> **TIP**
>
> **Most recent settings.** *The options on the Text workpane always show the settings you most recently used.*

Enter Text

1. Open the picture into which you want to insert text.

2. Click Text on the visual menu.

3. Click Insert Text on the Text menu.

4. Type the text that you want to enter.

5. While the text is still selected, change its font, size, and style by changing the options on the Text workpane, if you want.

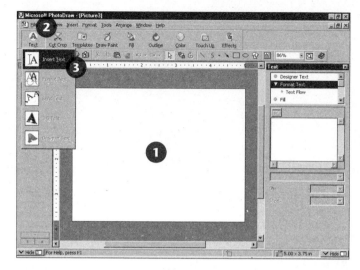

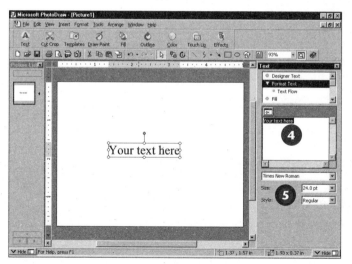

Formatting an Existing Text Object

You can change the formatting of any text object you have created. After you select the text object, you can change its options on the Text workpane.

> **TIP**
>
> **Selecting text objects.** *You can select a text object by opening the object list for the picture and then clicking the text object in the list.*

> **TIP**
>
> **Editing text shortcut.** *Rather than double-click a text object, you can select the object, click the right mouse button, and choose Edit Text from the shortcut menu.*

Change Text Font and Size

1 Double-click a text object on a picture or select the object from the object list for the picture.

2 Click Format Text in the workpane list.

3 Change the font, size, and style options.

Arranging Text Objects

Although most of the options for changing the appearance of text objects are on the Text workpane, you can also make changes (with greater flexibility in some cases) by manipulating the text object with the mouse. Among these changes are rotating a text object, resizing a text object, and stretching or compressing a text object to change the shape of the characters.

TIP

Changing line breaks. *To change where the lines of text break within a text object, click the object, and then, on the Text workpane, click in the text where you want the end of a line to be. Press Enter to insert a line break.*

Rotate Text Objects

1. Click a text object.

2. Drag the green rotation handle clockwise or counterclockwise around the text object.

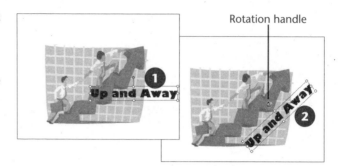

Rotation handle

Reshape Text Objects

1. Select the text object.

2. Drag a handle to resize or reshape the text.

   ◆ Drag a corner handle to resize the text object but maintain its shape.

   ◆ Drag a side, top, or bottom handle to reshape a text object.

Changing the Text Fill

Fills are the space within the strokes of characters. The edges of characters are their outlines. PhotoDraw offers five different fill types for text: solid color, texture, two types of gradient (a transition between colors), and picture. The rest of the fill-related settings on the Text workpane show options for the fill type that you choose. PhotoDraw displays options for textures and preset gradients in the gallery.

TIP

Matching colors. *To match a color from another picture, click the eyedropper on the workpane and then click the color on the picture. You can use this color as a solid color for a text object or for one of the colors in a gradient.*

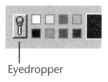

Eyedropper

Change the Fill

1. Insert a new text object or double-click an existing text object.

2. Click Fill in the workpane list.

3. In the Fill drop-down list, click a fill type.

4. Make selections on the Text workpane when options appear for the fill type.

6

Changing the Text Flow

The text flow options determine whether the lines of text in a text object are left-aligned, centered, or right-aligned within the text object, and whether the entire text object is rotated 90 degrees to the right, so it has a vertical rather than horizontal orientation.

TIP

Smoothing text. *As you follow these steps, you can clear the Smoothing check box on the Text workpane. The characters will gain sharper, but more jagged, edges.*

TRY THIS

Experiment with options. *Try different combinations of options on the Text workpane. Because you see the effects of your choices immediately, you can experiment and discover interesting new results.*

Change the Text Flow

1. Insert a new text object or double-click an existing text object.

2. Click Format Text in the workpane list if it is not already selected.

3. Click Text Flow in the workpane list.

4. Click the drop-down arrow next to the Align box and click an option in the Align list to change how the lines of text in a text object align.

5. Click the Vertical Orientation option if you want the text rotated 90 degrees clockwise.

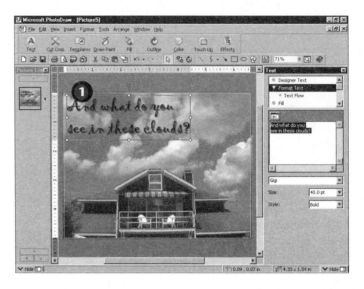

Bending Text

With PhotoDraw's Bend Text feature, you can create curved, and even circular, text for logos and other special uses. After you choose the type of bend you want, you can even determine the amount of the curvature, from slightly curved to a full circle.

When you choose to bend text, PhotoDraw shows a visual menu of bend options in the gallery on the Text workpane.

TIP

Unbending text. *To restore bent text to a flat, horizontal line, double-click the bent text, click Bend Text in the workpane list, and then click the No Bend button at the upper-left corner of the gallery.*

TIP

No Bend button. *The No Bend button looks like an "X."*

Bend Text

1 Insert a new text object or click an existing text object.

2 Click Text on the visual menu.

3 Click Bend Text on the Text menu.

4 On the workpane, click a bend shape in the gallery.

5 Drag the Amount slider to change the extent of the bend, from flat to fully circular.

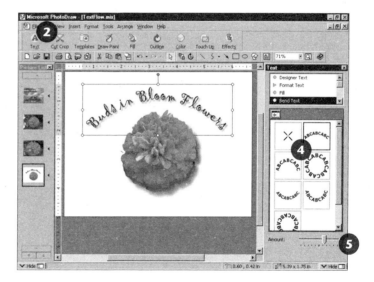

6

Changing the Edges of Characters

PhotoDraw offers a variety of ways to alter the edges of characters. In addition to choosing a contrasting color and particular width for character outlines, you can choose to have the outlines drawn with an artistic or photo brush. These brushes add a distinctive look to characters.

TRY THIS

Neat edges. *After you use an artistic or photo brush to create character outlines, remove the fill from characters by clicking Fill in the workpane list, clicking the drop-down arrow next to the display of colors, and then choosing No Fill from the list.*

SEE ALSO

For more information about changing the fill of characters, see "Changing the Text Fill" on page 51.

Change the Outline Color and Width

1. Insert a new text object or double-click an existing text object.

2. Click Outline in the workpane list.

3. Click Plain in the Gallery Type drop-down list.

4. Click a line style in the gallery.

5. Choose a color.

6. Drag the slider or enter a number in points to change the width of the character outlines.

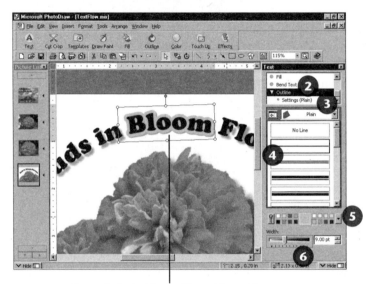

Separate text object with a wider outline

TIP

Seeing brushes. *To display the effects of Artistic and Photo Brushes, the text characters must be large enough to show the outlines clearly.*

SEE ALSO

For information about using Artistic and Photo Brushes, see "Changing the Edges of Characters" on page 54.

TIP

About points. *One inch equals 72 points.*

Choose an Artistic or Photo Brush

1. Insert a new text object or double-click an existing text object.

2. Click Outline in the workpane list.

3. Choose Artistic Brushes or Photo Brushes in the Gallery Type drop-down list.

4. Click a brush in the gallery.

5. Drag the Width slider or enter a number (in points) to change the width of the character outlines.

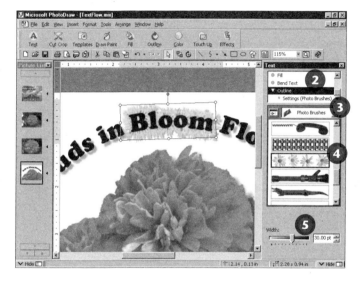

6

Choosing Designer Text

The designer text feature gives you a palette of complete looks that you can apply to text objects with a single click. When you use designer text, you don't have to worry about choosing a font, fill, outline, or bend. Each designer text type fills these settings out for you.

TIP

Going beyond designer text. *Designer text effects offer ready-made choices for everything on the Text workpane, but you can still modify individual aspects of the text, such as changing the photo brush used to draw the outlines.*

Select Designer Text

1. Insert a new text object or click an existing text object.

2. Click Text on the visual menu.

3. Click Designer Text on the Text menu.

4. Click a Designer Text style in the gallery.

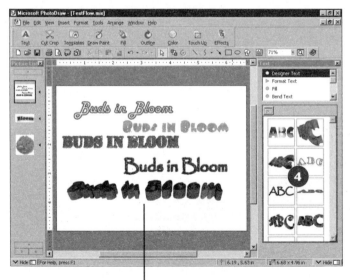

Designer text samples

Adding a Shadow to Text

You can use the same technique with a text object that you use to add a shadow to any object.

The transparency of a shadow determines how much objects underneath the shadow show through. The softness of a shadow determines how distinct its edges are.

TIP

Removing a shadow. *To remove a shadow, click the No Shadow button at the upper-left corner of the gallery of shadows on the Shadow workpane.*

TIP

Dragging the shadow into place. *The gallery offers preset shadow positions, but you can drag the shadow to any position by clicking the Shadow Position button on the Shadow workpane. This selects the shadow only. Drag the shadow to change its position.*

Add a Shadow

1. Insert a new text object or click an existing text object.

2. Click Effects on the visual menu.

3. Click Shadow on the Effects menu.

4. Click a shadow direction in the gallery on the Shadow workpane.

5. Choose a shadow color.

6. Drag the Transparency slider or enter a number to change the level of transparency in the shadow.

7. Drag the Soften slider or enter a number to change the softness at the edges of the shadow.

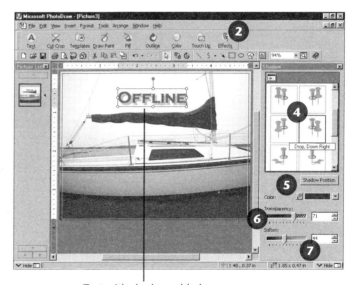

Text with shadow added

6

Making Text Fade Out

Faded text isn't text that's been washed too many times. It is text that is somewhat opaque at one end and transitions to being somewhat transparent. You can determine the percentage of transparency at either end of the fade-out. You can also determine the shape of the fade-out and its angle, and you can set the position of the fade-out's center, which determines how soon the fade effect begins as it develops across the text.

TIP

Getting the maximum effect. *For the maximum fade-out effect, set one transparency slider to 0% and the other to 100%.*

TRY THIS

Using a subtle fade. *Apply a subtle fade (less than 20%) from top to bottom or from bottom to top to give text a visual distinction.*

Fade Out Text

1. Insert a new text object or click an existing text object.

2. Click Effects on the visual menu.

3. Click Fade Out on the Effects menu.

4. Drag the Start or End slider or enter numbers in the percentage boxes to change the level of transparency at the start or end of the text object.

5. Use the Shape, Angle, and Center options on the Transparency workpane to fine-tune the appearance of the fade.

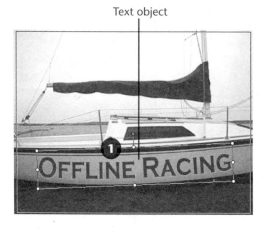

Text object

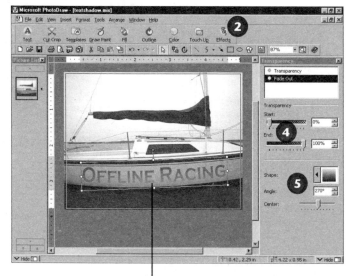

Text object with fade-out effect

Making Text Transparent

Rather than fade gradually from one end to the other, you can set a uniform transparency level to fade an entire text object. This allows you to superimpose text on another object, but still see the object through the text.

Make the Fill Transparent

1 Insert a new text object or click an existing text object.

2 Click Effects on the visual menu.

3 Click Transparency on the Effects menu.

4 On the Transparency workpane, drag the slider or enter a number in the percentage box to set the level of transparency.

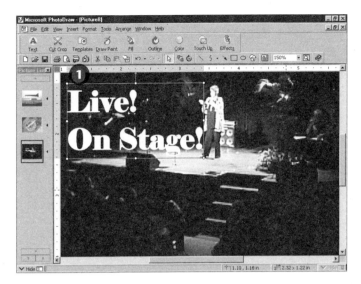

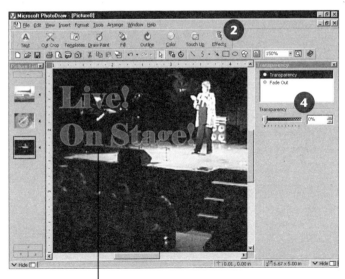

Text with transparency

6

Making Text 3-D

When you want truly distinctive text, you can go to the extreme and choose a preset designer 3-D text design or you can do something less extreme by simply applying some beveling or extrusion.

A designer 3-D text design has a full set of 3-D attributes, including rotation, tilt, and spot lighting that seems to emanate from particular points in space around the text. Text that is only beveled or extruded has the appearance of depth without the rotation, tilt, and custom lighting. A *bevel* is a chiseled edge. An *extrusion* gives characters in a text object depth by providing them with sides in addition to faces.

TRY THIS

Combining effects. *To push PhotoDraw to its limits, try applying a designer 3-D effect to text that you have bent with the Bend Text feature.*

Choose a 3-D Style

1. Insert a new text object or click an existing text object.

2. Click Text on the visual menu.

3. Click 3-D Text on the Text menu.

4. Click a 3-D text style in the gallery.

Text object given a 3-D text style

Choose a Bevel and Extrusion for Text

1. Insert a new text object or click an existing text object.

2. Click Text on the visual menu.

3. Click 3-D Text on the Text menu.

4. In the 3-D workpane list, click Beveling And Extrusion.

5. Click the Expand Gallery arrow on the workpane and click a bevel style.

6. Enter a depth and width for the bevel and extrusion.

Beveled and extruded text

Formatting 3-D Text

With the Rotate And Tilt option and the Lighting option on the 3-D workpane, you can alter advanced aspects of the 3-D designer effect that you have chosen. With these options, you can also enhance flat text or text to which you've applied only beveling and extrusion.

TIP

Back up before you begin.
Before you go wild with 3-D text, you may want to duplicate the text object so you have an unaltered backup. You can create several duplicates to try various combinations of 3-D options.

Rotate and Tilt the Text

1. Click the 3-D text.

2. Click Text on the visual menu.

3. Click 3-D Text on the Text menu.

4. Click Rotate And Tilt on the 3-D workpane.

5. Click the up or down arrows or enter numbers into the three rotation and tilt boxes.

Rotated and tilted text

Adding perspective. *The Lighting settings include a special option, Perspective, which lets you set whether the 3-D effect is relatively flat (little perspective distortion) or elongated (lots of perspective distortion).*

Change the Lighting

1. Click the 3-D text.

2. Click Text on the visual menu.

3. Click 3-D Text on the Text menu.

4. Click Lighting in the workpane list.

5. Click a preset lighting style in the gallery or click Settings for more options.

6. If you clicked Settings, click a light button labeled 1, 2, or 3 and then choose a color for the light. You can also change the tilt of the light with the two Tilt options.

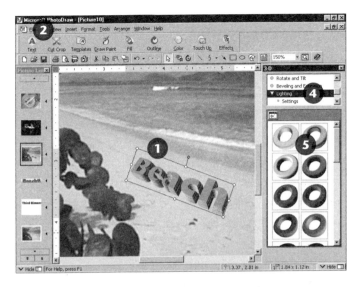

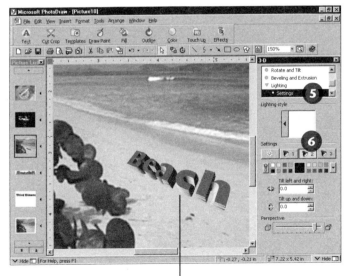

Text with lighting adjusted

6

Editing Individual Objects

One of the luxuries of using Microsoft PhotoDraw is that each object you add to a picture retains its individual shape, characteristics, and identity. In most programs that enable you to edit pictures, you work on areas of pixels, or screen dots, in a picture. The pixels may be discrete objects, but the larger shapes in the picture that they constitute are not. Shapes are just areas of pixels, so you can't easily choose particular shapes and give them shadows or add outlines, for example, without affecting other objects. These, on the other hand, are two quick and easy alterations that you can make in PhotoDraw.

In this section, you learn to make basic changes to the objects in a picture, such as altering their size and shape. These techniques require that you use the mouse to move handles, draw outlines, and drag shapes. In later sections, you learn to apply more sophisticated changes to objects, such as color modifications and designer effects.

Sizing an Object

You use the handles on objects to resize and reshape them. When you drag a handle at a corner, the object resizes and its shape stays the same. When you drag a side handle, or a handle at the top or bottom of a shape, you can distort the shape of an object, making it taller, shorter, narrower, or wider.

TIP

The mouse pointer shows the directions you can drag. *When you place the mouse pointer on a handle without clicking, the pointer becomes a set of arrows that shows the directions in which you can drag the handle.*

TIP

Resizing and reshaping objects outward from the center. *To resize or reshape objects from the center outward or inward, hold down the Ctrl key as you drag a handle.*

Drag an Object Larger or Smaller

1 Click an object.

2 Drag a handle to resize or reshape the object.

◆ Drag a corner handle to resize an object without changing its shape.

◆ Drag a side handle to reshape an object.

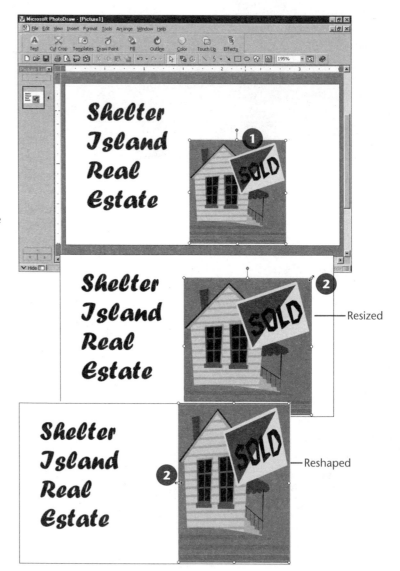

Resized

Reshaped

Specify an Exact Size

1 Click an object.

2 Click Arrange on the Arrange menu.

3 On the Arrange workpane, clear the Maintain Proportions check box if you want to change only the width or the height and not both simultaneously.

4 Change the Width and Height numbers and press Enter to resize the object.

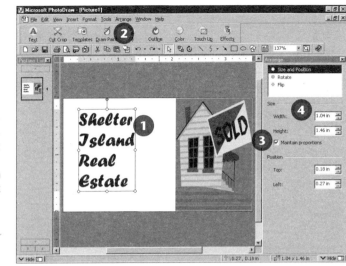

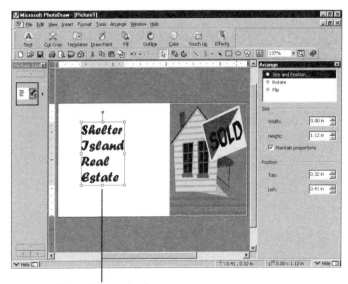

Text object resized

Positioning an Object

You can drag objects around a picture or you can position them by entering exact coordinates (in pixels) for their upper-left corners. The coordinate grid starts at the upper-left corner of the picture area so an object that is neatly aligned with the upper-left corner of the picture area is at Top=0, Left=0.

TRY THIS

Nudging an object with the arrow keys. *After you click an object, press an arrow key to nudge the object slightly. Press and hold the Shift key as you press an arrow key to move the object in larger increments.*

TIP

Setting the number of pixels per nudge. *To set the number of pixels the object moves when you press an arrow key, choose Options from the Tools menu and then click the General tab. You can change the Small Nudge and Large Nudge settings.*

Drag an Object to Position

1 Place the mouse pointer on an object.

2 Press and hold down the mouse button.

♦ Hold down the Shift key if you want to drag the object exactly horizontally or vertically.

3 Drag the object to a new position.

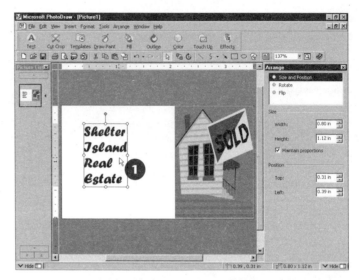

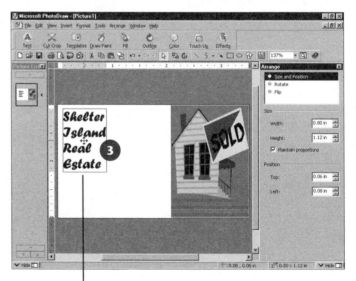

Object has been moved.

Making a quick copy of an object. *You can make a quick copy of an object by holding down the Ctrl key and dragging the object away from its current position. The original object stays in position, and a duplicate follows the mouse pointer.*

Checking an object's position. *Watch the status bar as you move an object. The left pair of numbers shows the object's position in pixels relative to the upper-left corner of the picture area. The first number in the pair shows the horizontal distance. The second number shows the vertical distance.*

Specify an Exact Position

1. Click an object.

2. Click Arrange on the Arrange menu.

3. Change the numbers in the Top and Left boxes to set the position of the upper-left corner of the object.

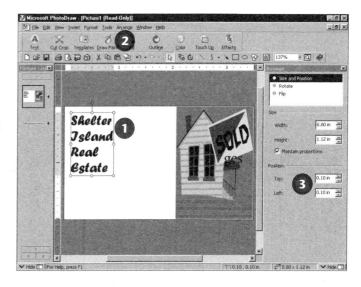

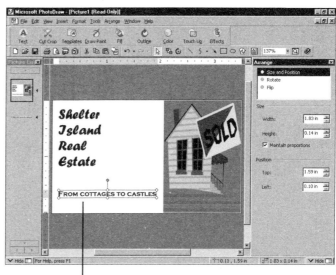

Text object given same
Left position setting as object above.

Rotating an Object

The quickest way to rotate an object is by dragging its rotation handle, but for more precision, you can enter an exact rotation angle. You can also enter an exact rotation angle to make sure that several objects are rotated to the same degree.

TIP

Rotating an object with more control. *To rotate an object with more control, click and hold down the mouse button on the rotation handle and drag the mouse pointer away from the object. Then drag the mouse pointer around the object.*

TRY THIS

Spinning out of control. *Place the mouse pointer on an object's rotation handle and then drag to the center of the object. Drag the mouse pointer around in a small circle to quickly spin the object and make yourself nauseous.*

Spin an Object Using the Rotation Handle

1. Click an object.

2. Position the mouse pointer on the object's green rotation handle.

3. Press and hold down the mouse button and drag the rotation handle in a circle around the object, either clockwise or counterclockwise.

4. Release the mouse button when the object is rotated the way you want.

Rotation handle

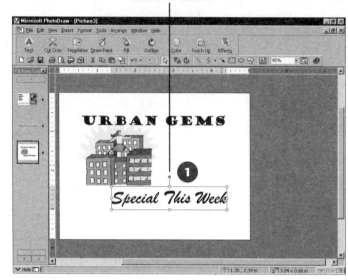

TIP

Rotating multiple objects.
You can select multiple objects and then rotate them. Each rotates around its own center.

TIP

Rotating multiple objects around their collective center. *To rotate a group of objects around their collective center, group them and then rotate the group.*

SEE ALSO

For more information about grouping objects, see "Grouping Objects" on page 137.

Choose a Rotation Angle

1 Click an object.

2 Click the Custom Rotate button on the toolbar.

3 Use one of the following methods.

◆ Click one of the preset rotation angles in the gallery.

◆ Type a rotation angle in the Custom box below the gallery.

Custom Rotate button

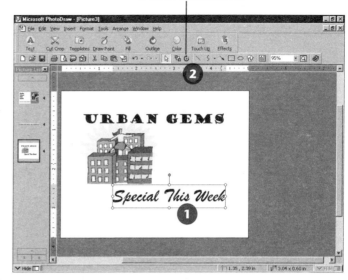

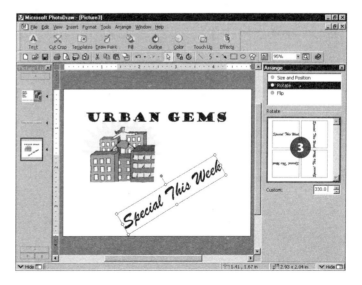

Flipping an Object

Flipping isn't just for short-order cooks. It's a PhotoDraw technique you can use to switch the sides of an object from left to right or from top to bottom.

TIP

Using the Flip commands on the menu. *After you select an object, you can also point to Flip on the Arrange menu and then choose the Flip Horizontal, Flip Vertical, and Flip Both commands.*

TIP

Checking an item in the gallery. *Remember, to see a description of an item in the gallery, place the mouse pointer on it without clicking and pause.*

TRY THIS

Creating facing objects. *To quickly make two identical objects face each other, press Ctrl as you drag off a copy of an object, align the two objects, and then flip one of them.*

Flip Horizontally or Vertically

1. Click an object.

2. Click the Custom Rotate button on the toolbar.

3. In the workpane list, click Flip.

4. Click one of the four preset flip directions in the gallery.

Custom Rotate button

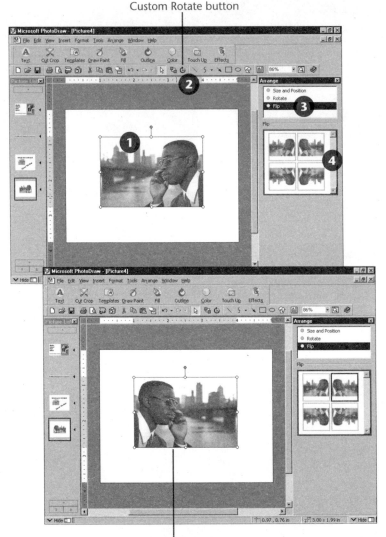

Picture flipped

Skewing an Object

By skewing an object, you can make it appear to lean. A skewed rectangle is a parallelogram, for example. As there is no Skew command, you can only accomplish skewing by using the keyboard in conjunction with the mouse.

The skew feature works well for any object you create in PhotoDraw. You can even use it to skew photos.

> **TIP**
>
> **Skewing text.** *You can skew text to make it look like it's on the side of an object.*

> **TIP**
>
> **Going beyond the skew.** *For more interesting permutations, try applying a distortion effect to an object. For more information about using distortions, see "Adding a Distort Effect" on page 116.*

Skew an Object

1 Click an object.

2 Press and hold the Ctrl and Alt keys on the keyboard.

3 Click a handle on one of the object's sides, and then drag it perpendicular to the direction of the mouse pointer arrows. For example, if the mouse pointer arrows point up and down, drag the handle left or right.

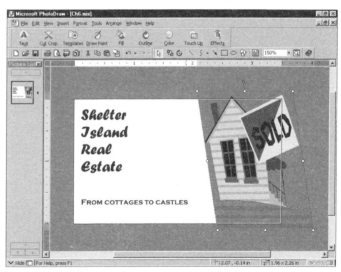

Cropping an Object

You don't have to use scissors to cut away the part of a picture that you don't want. In PhotoDraw, you can use the Crop feature. You choose a crop pattern to place on the picture like a stencil. The part of the picture that is within the pattern is kept, and the rest is removed.

TIP

Crop vs. Cut Out. *To draw your own crop pattern, cut out an area by color, or cut out a subject by selecting its outlines, use the Cut Out feature, instead.*

SEE ALSO

For more information about the Cut Out feature, see "Cutting Out a Shape" on page 75.

TRY THIS

Fitting a crop pattern. *You can click Stretch To Fit on the Crop workpane to have the pattern stretched to fit neatly on the picture.*

Choose a Crop Pattern

1. Click an object.

2. Click the Cut Crop button on the visual menu.

3. Click Crop on the Cut Crop menu.

4. Click a crop pattern in the gallery.

5. Drag the handles of the superimposed crop pattern object to change the size, shape, and rotation of the crop pattern.

6. Click Finish to preview how the crop looks.

7. Click None if you want to remove the current crop and try a different crop pattern.

8. Click Lock Crop to finalize the crop when you are satisfied with the appearance of the crop.

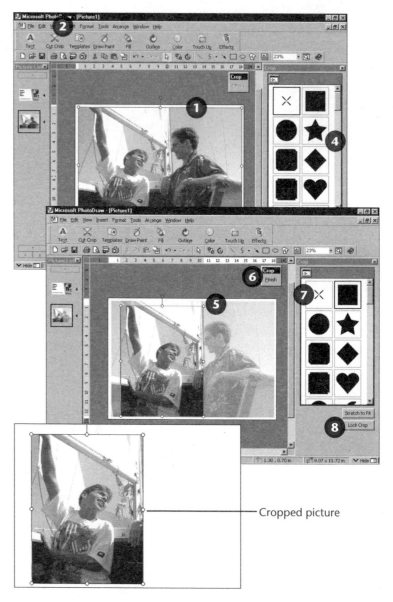

Cropped picture

Cutting Out a Shape

Using Cut Out is similar to cropping, but it lets you extract an area of a picture and put it in a new object. You can determine the softness of the edge of the cutout shape, and whether the area that you cut out is put into a new picture or left in the current picture. Also, when you use Cut Out, you can choose to cut out the opposite area, which means that the area outside the shape is removed rather than the area within the shape.

TIP

Transparency surrounding a cutout. *When you cut out a shape, the area outside the borders of the shape becomes transparent. Objects that are underneath this area become visible.*

Cut Out a Shape

1. Click an object.

2. Click the Cut Crop button on the visual menu and click Cut Out on the Cut Crop menu.

3. Click By Shape in the workpane list.

4. Click a shape in the gallery.

5. Drag the Edge slider toward Soft if you want the cutout edge to be softer.

6. Click the Cut Out Opposite Area check box to put the area *outside* the shape in a new object. Clear the Put In New Picture check box if you want the shape to stay in the current picture as a new object.

7. Drag the handles on the cutout shape to change its size, shape, position, or rotation.

8. Click Finish.

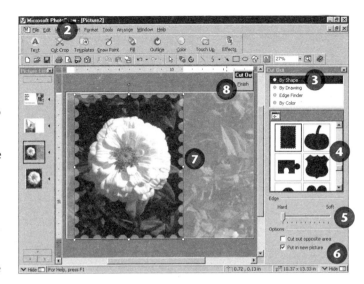

New picture

Drawing an Area to Cut Out

Rather than use a standard shape to define an area to cut out, you can draw your own freeform shape.

After you draw a shape, you see a highlighted preview of it. Before you commit to the cutout by clicking Finish, you can reshape the shape by dragging segments one by one.

> **TIP**
>
> **Reversing course.** *As you draw segments of the shape, you can click Undo Last on the floating Cut Out toolbar to remove the last segment.*

> **TIP**
>
> **Starting over.** *To start over, click the Reset button on the floating Cut Out toolbar.*

Draw a Cutout

1. Click an object.

2. Click the Cut Crop button on the visual menu and click Cut Out from the Cut Crop menu.

3. Click By Drawing in the workpane list.

4. Place the mouse pointer on the picture at the start of the shape you will draw.

5. Drag the mouse pointer to draw shapes, or click spots to connect with straight lines.

6. Click the the yellow diamond to finish.

7. Drag the Path Smoothness slider to give the cutout a softer edge.

8. Click Cut Out Opposite Area to cut out the area *outside* the shape. Clear the Put In New Picture check box to keep the shape in the picture.

9. Click Finish.

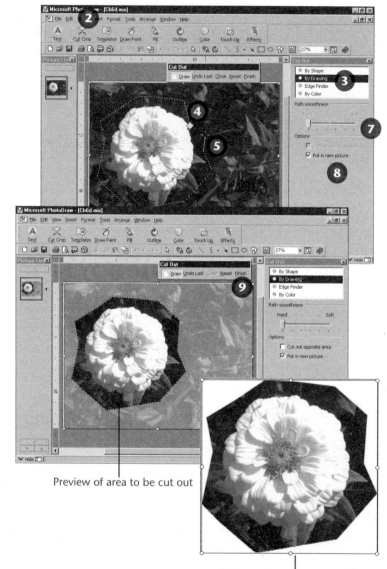

Preview of area to be cut out

Cutout picture in a new object

TIP

Sprouting segments. *When you drag a segment, you create two segments that intersect at the point where you clicked. You can then reshape these two segments individually.*

TIP

Moving two segments. *To move two segments, place the mouse pointer on the spot where the segments meet. Both segments are highlighted.*

TIP

Closing a shape. *To join the last point with the first point that you drew, click the Close button on the floating Cut Out toolbar.*

Modify the Shape of the Area You Have Drawn

① Draw an area to cut out (follow the procedure on the opposite page), but do not click Finish.

② Place the mouse pointer on any point on a segment along the outline of the shape or on the point at the intersection of two segments.

③ Drag the point.

④ Drag other points, if necessary, until the shape is the way you want.

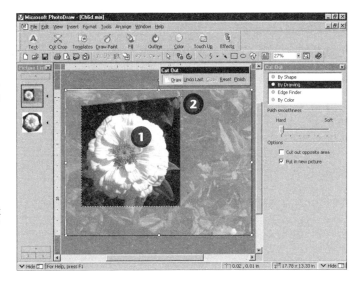

Finding an Area to Cut Out

If an area that you want to cut out of a picture has distinct edges or a uniform color, you can use special techniques for finding the area to cut out. The edge finder detects the boundary between two areas in a picture if the contrast between brightness or color is sufficient. If the area that you want to cut out is a different color from the rest of the picture, you can find it by color. This works well when the subject of a picture has been photographed against a monochromatic background, such as a white wall.

TIP

Narrowing in on the edge.
Changing the edge finder width allows you to use a narrow edge finder rectangle and select the area in which to detect the edge with more precision.

Find the Edge

1. Click an object.

2. Click the Cut Crop button on the visual menu and click Cut Out on the Cut Crop menu.

3. Click Edge Finder in the workpane list.

4. Click an Edge Finder width.

5. Click the edge of the area to cut out.

6. Move the mouse pointer along the edge, keeping the edge within the rectangle.

7. Click again and move the mouse pointer further along the edge.

8. Continue clicking and complete the shape by clicking the yellow diamond.

9. Drag segments of the outline of the shape to fine-tune the shape and then click Finish to cut out the highlighted area.

Cut Out According to Color

1 Click an object.

2 Click the Cut Crop button on the visual menu and click Cut Out on the Cut Crop menu.

3 Click By Color in the workpane list.

4 Drag the Color Matching slider toward More to narrow the range of color that is selected.

5 Drag the Edge slider toward Soft to soften the cutout edge.

6 Change the Search Mode to Global if you want to find all areas of the same color, even non-adjacent areas.

7 Click the color to find in the picture.

8 Click another color or another shade of the current color to add it to the selection.

9 Click Finish.

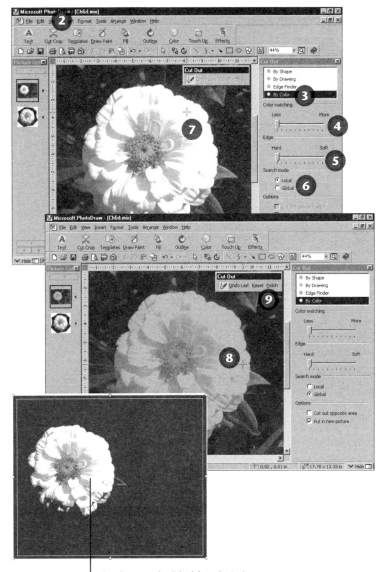

Cutout area (gray background added for clarity)

Erasing Part of an Object

Using Erase is exactly the opposite of using Cut Out. Rather than extracting and preserving an area of a picture, Erase removes it. In fact, if you choose Erase Opposite Area, you get the same result as using Cut Out.

You use the same techniques to erase as you do to cut out. You can erase shapes, draw shapes to erase, find areas to erase with the Edge Finder, and erase certain colors.

TIP

More pleasing pictures.
People who routinely cut themselves out of pictures can use the erase techniques, instead.

SEE ALSO

For more information about related cut out techniques, see "Drawing an Area to Cut Out" on page 76 and "Finding an Area to Cut Out" on page 78.

Erase a Shape

1. Click an object.

2. Click the Cut Crop button on the visual menu and click Erase on the Cut Crop menu.

3. Click By Shape in the workpane list.

4. Click a shape in the gallery.

5. Drag the Edge slider toward Soft if you want the edge of the erased area to be softer.

6. Click the Erase Opposite Area check box if you want to erase the area *outside* the shape.

7. Drag the handles on the superimposed cutout shape to change its size, shape, position, or rotation.

8. Click Finish.

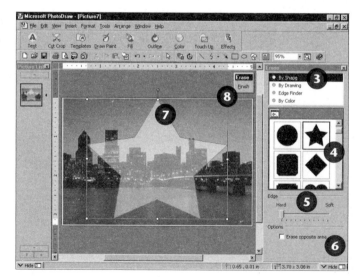

Fine-tuning a shape. *After you draw a shape to erase, you can fine-tune the shape by placing the mouse pointer on the outline of the shape and dragging points. A new point is created wherever you click on the outline.*

Seeing underlying objects. *The area that you erase becomes transparent. If you erase part of an object that overlaps another object, you can see the underlying object in the erased area.*

Draw a Shape to Erase

1. Click an object.

2. Click the Cut Crop button on the Visual menu toolbar and choose Erase from the Cut Crop menu.

3. Click By Drawing.

4. Place the mouse pointer at the start of the shape to draw.

5. Drag the mouse pointer to draw free-form shapes, or click spots that you want to connect with straight lines.

6. Complete the shape by clicking the yellow diamond.

7. Drag the Path Smoothness slider toward Soft to give the edge of the erased area a softer edge.

8. Click the Erase Opposite Area check box if you want to erase the area *outside* the shape.

9. Click Finish.

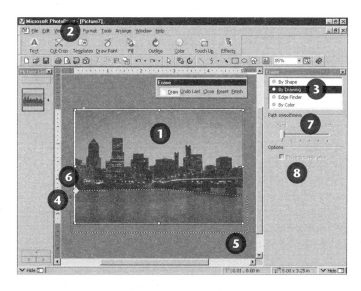

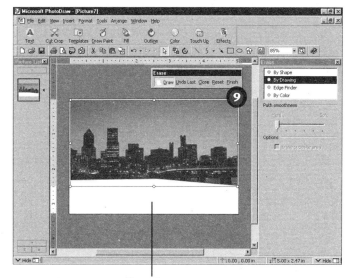

Erased area

Choosing an Area to Erase

As with Erase By Shape and Erase By Drawing, erasing with the edge finder and Erase By Color are similar but the opposite of their counterparts on the Cut Out workpane. The areas that PhotoDraw finds according to your choices are erased from the picture rather than saved.

TIP

Zoom while you work. *You can zoom in while you are using the edge finder to make it easier to see your work.*

SEE ALSO

For more information about the related cut out techniques, see "Finding an Area to Cut Out" on page 78.

Find the Edge

1. Click an object.

2. Click the Cut Crop button in the visual menu and click Erase on the Cut Crop menu.

3. Click Edge Finder.

4. Click an Edge Finder width.

5. Click the edge of the area to erase.

6. Move the mouse pointer along the edge, keeping the edge within the rectangle.

7. Click again and move the mouse pointer farther along the edge.

8. Continue clicking and then click the yellow diamond to complete the shape.

9. Drag segments along the outline of the previewed shape to fine-tune the shape, and then click Finish to erase the highlighted area.

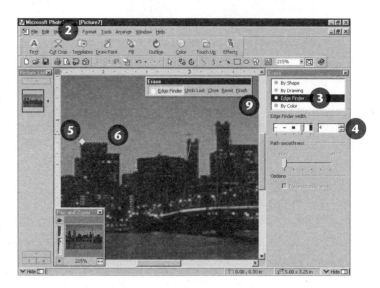

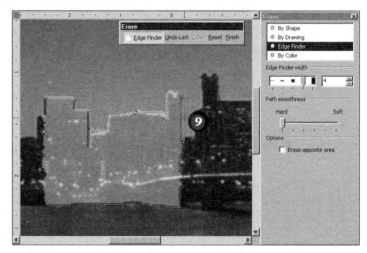

TIP

Proceeding after undoing an erase. *If you undo an erase operation and want to try again, you must click the Drag Path button on the floating Erase toolbar before you can click another color area on the image.*

Erase an Area According to Color

1. Click an object.

2. Click the Cut Crop button on the visual menu and click Erase on the Cut Crop menu.

3. Click By Color in the workpane list.

4. Drag the Color Matching slider toward More to narrow the range of color that is selected.

5. Drag the Edge slider toward Soft to soften the edge.

6. Choose Global search mode to find the color in non-adjacent areas.

7. Click the color in the picture that you want to find.

8. Click another color or another shade of the current color to add it to the selection.

9. Click Finish.

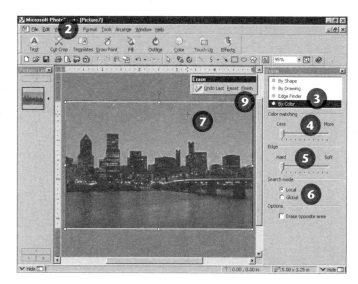

8

Working with Color

Few graphics programs give you as much control over color as Microsoft PhotoDraw. You can fill shapes that you've drawn or painted with simple, single-color fills, or you can choose to fill an object with a much more elaborate two-color gradient or one of PhotoDraw's many designer gradients, which provide sophisticated patterns of color.

In addition to applying whole new colors to objects, you can make more subtle changes to the coloration within objects, especially photos. You can change the tint within photos to reduce or increase the amount of a particular color, you can color balance a photo to rectify color problems, and you can change the hue and saturation of colors in a photo to compensate for faded photos or scans. You can also use PhotoDraw's color tools to achieve creative, artistic effects by colorizing photos, turning them into negatives, and converting them to grayscale images that look like black and white photos.

Changing the Color of an Object

The space within an object is its *fill*. To change the color of an object, whether that object is a shape you've drawn or an image, you can give it a different fill color.

TIP

Fill on the Formatting toolbar. *If the Formatting toolbar is turned on, you can click the drop-down arrow next to the Fill Color button and quickly select a fill color from a color palette.*

TIP

Removing the fill. *To remove a fill, click the drop-down arrow next to the color chips on the Fill workpane, and click No Fill.*

Change the Fill Color

1. Click the object.

2. Click Fill on the visual menu.

3. Click Solid Color on the Fill menu.

4. Choose a basic color by clicking one of the eight, small color chips to the *left* of the large chip that shows the current color.

5. Choose a shade of the basic color you've selected by clicking one of the eight, small color chips to the *right* of the large chip that shows the current color.

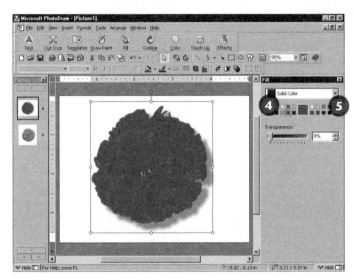

The go-anywhere eye-dropper. *The eyedropper can pick up color from anywhere on the screen, even from within the windows of other programs. You can click a color in the Microsoft FrontPage or Microsoft PowerPoint window, for example, to pick up a color from a Web page design or a presentation.*

Making fills partially transparent. *In addition to selecting a color to fill an object, you can also select a transparency level for the color by dragging the Transparency slider on the Fill workpane. Increasing the transparency lets the background beneath an object show through.*

Pick Up a Color with the Eyedropper

1. Open a picture that has the color you want.

2. Select a different object to fill.

3. Click Fill on the visual menu.

4. Click Solid Color on the Fill menu.

5. Click the Eyedropper on the Fill workpane.

6. Click the color on the picture that you want to use to fill the second object.

Eyedropper

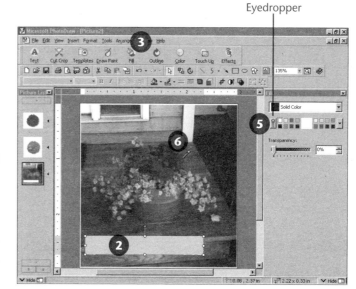

Object has been filled.

8

Filling Objects with Gradients

When you fill an object with a gradient, the color in the object changes from one side to the other, from top to bottom, from the center to the edge, or in other, more complex patterns.

You can create a basic, two-color gradient, which starts at one color and ends at another, or you can pick a more sophisticated pattern of colors from the palette of designer gradients.

TIP

Designer gradients and outlines. *When you fill an object with a designer gradient, the gradient extends out onto the outline of the object, too. In other words, the width of the outline is filled by the gradient in addition to the regular interior space of the object.*

Choose a Designer Gradient

1. Click the object.

2. Click Fill on the visual menu.

3. Click Designer Gradient on the Fill menu.

4. Click a gradient on the gallery.

5. If you want objects underneath the gradient to show through, drag the Transparency slider to the right.

6. To change the shape of the gradient, click the Expand Gallery (left arrow) button to open the gallery, and then click a shape in the gallery.

7. To change the angle at which the gradient runs, click the up or down arrow next to the Angle box.

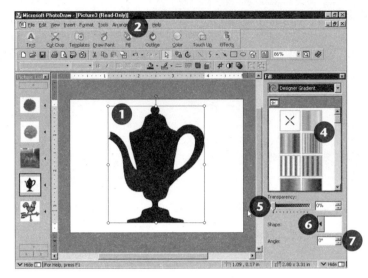

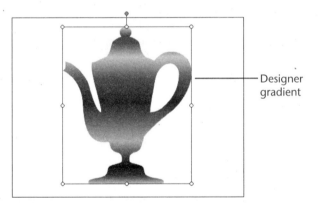

Designer gradient

Create a Two-Color Gradient

1. Click the object.

2. Click Fill on the visual menu.

3. Click Two-Color Gradient on the Fill menu.

4. Select a Start color and transparency.

5. Select an End color and transparency.

6. Click the Expand Gallery (left arrow) button to open the gallery of shapes, and then click a shape in the gallery.

7. To change the angle at which the gradient runs, enter an angle into the Angle box or click the up and down arrows next to the Angle box to make small adjustments.

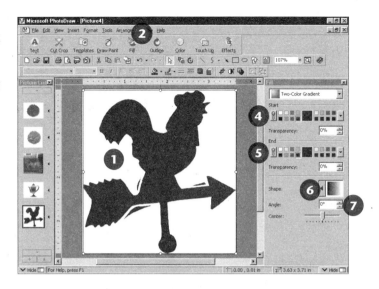

Using Color Palettes

In addition to the standard eight colors (and eight variations of each color) that you can click on many workpanes, PhotoDraw offers several color palettes from which you can choose a broader array of colors. The True Color palette displays all the colors the human eye can differentiate (more than 16 million colors). The Web palette offers a 256-color subset of the True Color palette that are the colors that can be displayed by Web browsers (also known as the "browser-safe" palette).

> **TIP**
>
> **Using the True Color pop-out menu.** *In addition to viewing the True Color tab, as described in the procedure on this page, you can open the True Color pop-out menu and point to a color. At step 2 in the following procedure, point to True Color rather than click More Colors.*

Use the True Color Palette

1. On any workpane that shows color chips, click the drop-down arrow button next to the color chips.

2. Click More Colors.

3. Click the True Color tab in the More Colors dialog box.

4. Drag the small circle to the color you want on the color matrix. You can also enter values in the Red, Green, and Blue boxes to reproduce a specific color.

5. Click OK.

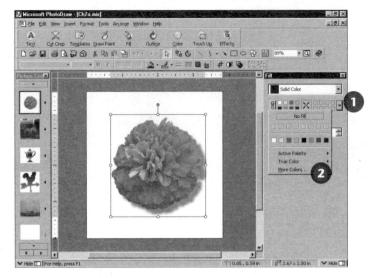

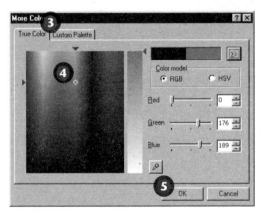

Use the Web Palette

1. On any workpane that shows color chips, click the drop-down arrow button next to the color chips.

2. Click More Colors.

3. On the Custom Palette tab of the More Colors dialog box, click the drop-down arrow button next to the Color Palette box.

4. Choose Web (Dithered) or Web (Solid).

5. Click a color on the color grid.

6. Click OK.

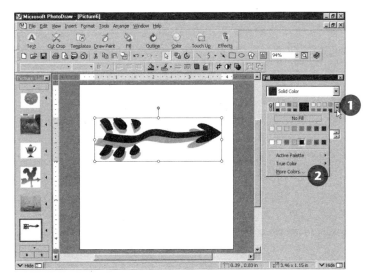

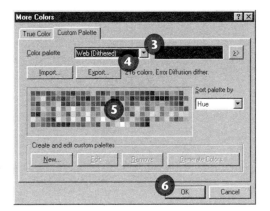

Converting an Object to Grayscale

Converting an object to grayscale changes it from color to shades of gray. The grayscale image looks like a black and white photograph. The lighter colors in the original image become lighter grays and the darker colors become darker grays.

Making an image appear to transition from black and white to color. *It's the Wizard of Oz effect. To make an image transition from black and white (actually, grayscale) to color, duplicate the image and make one of the copies grayscale. Apply the Fade Out effect to the color image and place it precisely on top of the grayscale copy.*

For more information about the Fade Out effect, see "Giving a Fade to a Picture" on page 115.

Convert to Grayscale

1. Click the object.

2. Click Color on the visual menu.

3. Click Grayscale on the Color menu.

4. Click the Grayscale button on the Color workpane.

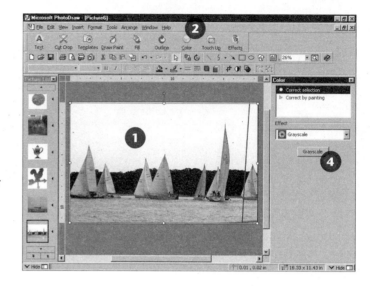

Tinting a Photo

With PhotoDraw's Tint command, you can increase or reduce the amount of a particular color in an image. This can be helpful, for example, when you want to correct a photo that has been exposed to sunlight for too long by increasing the color that has faded.

Change the Tint

1. Click the photo.

2. Click Color on the visual menu.

3. Click Tint on the Color menu.

4. Drag the Hue slider to the color you want.

5. Drag the Amount slider left or right to decrease or increase the hue you've chosen.

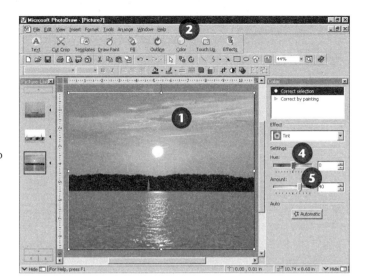

Colorizing a Photo

By colorizing a photo, you can replace its colors with shades of a single color that you choose. Colorizing is much like converting a color photo to grayscale, except that the photo becomes shades of a color rather than shades of gray. Lighter colors become lighter shades of a color and darker colors become darker shades of the same color.

TRY THIS

Creating an old-fashioned look. *Try using the Colorize command and choose a dull orange as the color. Lights and darks in the photo will be mapped to light and dark oranges, and the color will take on an old-fashioned sepia-toned look.*

Colorize a Photo

1 Click the photo.

2 Click Color on the visual menu.

3 Click Colorize on the Color menu.

4 Click a color chip on the workpane or click the drop-down arrow next to the color chips and choose a color from one of the color palettes on the menu.

5 Drag the Amount slider to the right to increase the amount of colorization.

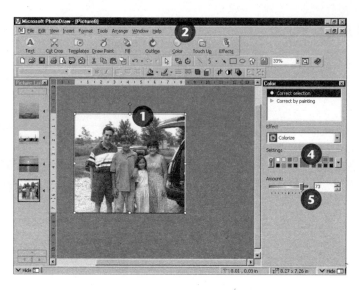

Changing the Color Balance in a Photo

To make subtle shifts in the colors of a photo, you can use the Color Balance option, which lets you change the balance between three pairs of colors. As you increase one color in a pair, the opposite color decreases.

Change the Color Balance

1. Click the photo.

2. Click Color on the visual menu.

3. Click Color Balance on the Color menu.

4. Drag one or more of the three sliders on the workpane left or right to change the balance between the colors in the three color pairs.

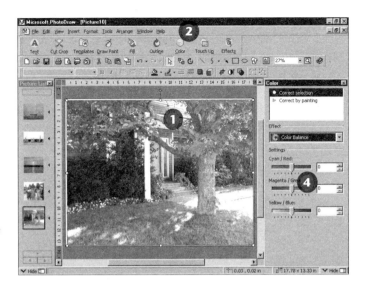

8

Changing the Hue and Saturation in a Photo

Unlike the Colorize command, which applies color to the overall image (including areas of gray, black, and white), changing the hue and saturation affects only the colors in a photo, not the gray shades. It shifts them around a virtual color wheel (a circular rainbow) and changes the intensity of the colors.

> **TIP**
>
> **Sliders provide visual clues.** *The sliders show the current color setting.*

> **TIP**
>
> **Color brightness.** *Unlike the Brightness And Contrast option on the Color menu, the Brightness setting on the Color workpane allows you to change the lightness and darkness of the colors in an image without affecting the gray shades.*

Adjust the Hue and Saturation

1 Click the photo.

2 Click Color on the visual menu.

3 Click Hue And Saturation on the Color menu.

4 Drag the Hue slider to adjust the color.

5 Drag the Saturation slider to adjust the intensity of the hue that you have chosen.

6 Drag the Brightness slider to adjust the brightness of the colors in the image.

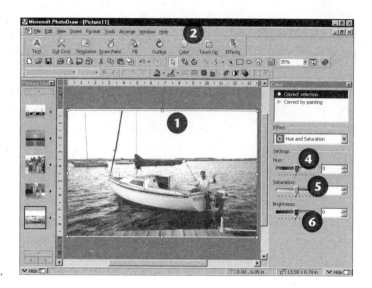

Creating a Negative

Other than converting an image to grayscale, creating a negative is the easiest color-related task to accomplish. You won't be doing it every day, but creating a negative can provide an interesting artistic effect for use in a composition or collage.

Create a Negative

1. Click the photo.

2. Click Color on the visual menu.

3. Click Negative on the Color menu.

4. Click the Negative button on the Color workpane.

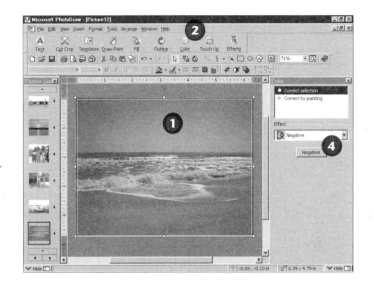

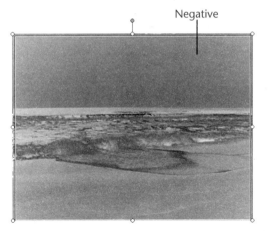

Negative

9

Touching Up Photos

Even when your composition is perfect, your subject is interesting, and your photographic technique is flawless, Microsoft PhotoDraw's image retouching capabilities can help you compensate for the vicissitudes of your digital camera or scanner. They can change the brightness or contrast in a picture and remove speckles and dust. They can also fix photos that are spotted or scratched, or remove that all-too-familiar red-eye glow you often see in photos taken with a flash. PhotoDraw can even help you alter reality by painting over something undesirable (like finger antennae behind someone's head) with another part of the same picture (a little bit of that lovely wallpaper you put up last year).

Brightening a Picture and Changing the Contrast

Not all scanners and digital cameras can capture the full range of contrast in a photo or scene, so the images they produce can look dull.

You can use PhotoDraw's Brightness And Contrast options to make photos more vivid by adjusting the levels manually or letting Photo-Draw determine appropriate levels.

TIP

Restoring original colors.
If you are unsatisfied with the changes you've made, you can either click Undo or use Restore to restore an object's original colors. To use Restore, click any option on the Color menu and choose Restore from the Effect list on the workpane. Then click the Restore button on the workpane.

Use Automatic Brightness and Contrast

1 Select the photo.

2 Click Color on the visual menu.

3 Click Brightness And Contrast on the Color menu.

4 Click Automatic on the Color workpane.

Brightness and contrast are adjusted automatically.

Change the Brightness and Contrast

1. Select the photo.

2. Click Color on the visual menu.

3. Click Brightness And Contrast on the Color menu.

4. Drag the Brightness and Contrast sliders to the right or left to increase or decrease these settings.

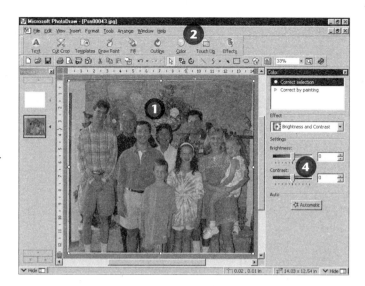

Brightness and color are adjusted manually.

Fixing Red Eye

Do your flash photos make your friends and family look like demons? Fortunately, PhotoDraw can remove red eye, that glowing red color that often appears in the eyes of people photographed with flash bulbs. With PhotoDraw's Fix Red Eye feature, people will no longer scream when they see themselves in your photos.

TRY THIS

When Fix Red Eye doesn't work. *When automatic red eye removal doesn't work completely, you can try Manual Red Eye. After you choose Fix Red Eye from the Touch Up menu, click Manual Red Eye in the workpane list. Draw a circle around the red eye and click the yellow diamond where you started. Click Fix in the floating Manual Red Eye dialog box and then click either Reset or Finish.*

Fix Red Eye

1. Select the photo.

2. Zoom in on the eyes by clicking the Pan And Zoom button, dragging up the slider on the Pan And Zoom dialog box, and dragging the red outline around the eyes.

3. Click Touch Up on the visual menu.

4. Click Fix Red Eye on the Touch Up menu.

5. Click the red part of the eye in the photo.

6. Click Fix in the floating Red Eye dialog box.

7. Click Reset if you want to try again or click Finish to accept the change.

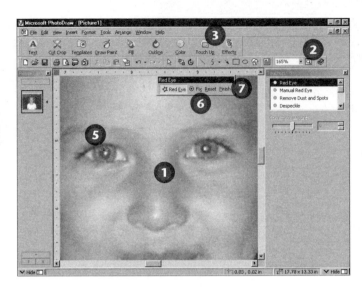

Removing Dust and Spots

Sometimes dust too fine to see on a photo shows up vividly in a scan. At other times, objects in the background of a photo pick up extra light and sparkle.

PhotoDraw lets you click spots, either light or dark, and smooth them over. The spot you click blends into its surroundings and becomes unnoticeable.

TRY THIS

Digital airbrushing. *The Remove Dust And Spots feature works equally well with any type of spot, even freckles on faces and those dreaded age spots.*

Remove Dust and Spots

1. Click the photo.

2. Zoom in on the dust or spot that you want to remove.

3. Click Touch Up on the visual menu.

4. Click Remove Dust And Spots on the Touch Up menu.

5. Click each dust particle or spot that you want to remove.

6. If you want, click Undo Last on the floating Dust And Spots dialog box to restore the last spot you removed.

7. When you're done, click Finish.

Spots are removed.

Removing Scratches

Older photos often have large and obvious scratches that you want to remove. Even new photos can have small scratches that show up vividly after they are scanned.

PhotoDraw's Remove Scratch feature makes it especially easy to remove a scratch. The scratch is blended into the background so it becomes invisible.

TIP

Removing fine lines. *In addition to removing scratches, you can use the Remove Scratch command to remove any unwanted fine line in a photo, such as a power line across an outdoor landscape photo.*

Remove a Scratch

1. Click the photo.

2. Zoom in on the scratch.

3. Click Touch Up on the visual menu.

4. Click Remove Scratch on the Touch Up menu.

5. Click one of the Scratch Width options.

6. Click at the beginning of the scratch and move the mouse pointer to stretch the scratch removal box along a segment of the scratch, making sure the box covers the segment.

7. Click again.

8. Continue along the scratch, removing segment after segment, until the scratch is entirely removed.

9. Click Finish.

Segment of scratch is fixed.

Sharpening and Blurring a Photo

Sharpening a photo can appear to give it a little better focus. The opposite of sharpening, blurring, can soften a photo.

Sharpen a photo sparingly because sharpening a photo also enhances edges in the image and it can impart an undesirable graininess.

TRY THIS

Enhancing a photo's central subject. *Cut out the central figure of a photo and put it in a new picture. Blur the original photo a little and then drag back in the central figure that you cut out. When you place the central figure back into its original picture, it will gain focus and the background will lose focus.*

Sharpen or Blur a Photo

1. Click the photo.

2. Click Effects on the visual menu.

3. Click Blur And Sharpen on the Effects menu.

4. Drag the Blur/ Sharpen slider to the right to sharpen the image or to the left to blur the image.

Cloning Part of a Photo

With cloning, you can pick up one part of an image and paint it on a different part. This allows you to duplicate (clone) a part of a picture and place it on top of something else that is unwanted. You can clone an area of trees in one part of a landscape and cover the toxic waste dump in a different part.

TIP

Painting outside an object.
You can clone a part of a picture and paint it outside the frame of the picture. The picture automatically expands to include the area you are painting.

Clone

1 Click the photo.

2 Click Touch Up on the visual menu.

3 Click Clone on the Touch Up menu.

4 Drag the Amount slider left or right to change the transparency level of the area you will paint.

5 Click the Expand Gallery button next to the Brush setting to view and choose a different brush style with which to paint the cloned image.

6 Click the picture to pick up a part of the picture in the shape of the brush, and release the mouse button.

7 Hold down the mouse button and drag the mouse pointer across a different part of the picture to paint the cloned image.

8 Click Undo Last to back up a step or click Finish.

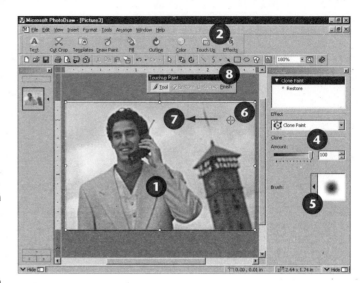

Part of sky cloned to cover pole

Smudging Part of a Photo

With smudging, you can push color around a picture the same way you pushed finger paints around a painting as a child. Smudging helps you smooth over small blemishes or blur the distinction between items in a picture. You may want to zoom in on the area that you want to smudge.

TIP

Unsmudging a picture.
PhotoDraw remembers the original picture. You can click Restore in the workpane list and then unsmudge an area by dragging in the opposite direction until the smudge is removed.

Smudge

1. Click the photo.

2. Click Touch Up on the visual menu.

3. Click Smudge on the Touch Up menu.

4. Drag the Amount slider if you want to reduce the degree of smudging that will occur.

5. Click the Expand Gallery button next to the Brush setting to view and choose a brush style with which to smudge the image.

6. Place the mouse pointer on the picture, hold down the mouse button, and drag in the direction you want to smudge the image.

7. Continue smudging until you are satisfied.

8. Click Finish.

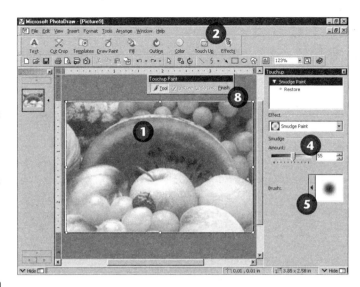

Watermelon seeds are removed.

Erasing Part of a Photo

Using the Erase option on the Touch Up menu is like dragging across a real drawing with an actual eraser, but the area that you erase in Photo-Draw becomes transparent. Objects that are underneath show through.

Unlike Erase on the Cut Crop menu, which allows you to draw precise areas to remove, the Erase feature on the Touch Up menu allows you to erase areas by painting across them.

TRY THIS

Erasing in real time. *While dragging the erase brush, pause a moment and the stroke that you've painted with the erase brush is erased.*

Erase

1. Click the photo.

2. Click Touch Up on the visual menu.

3. Click Erase on the Touch Up menu.

4. Drag the Amount slider left or right to change the amount of transparency you will add by erasing areas.

5. Click the Expand Gallery button next to the Brush setting to view and choose a brush style with which to erase part of the image.

6. Drag across the area to erase.

7. Click Undo Last to reverse the last stroke or click Finish.

Text added in erased area

Despeckling a Photo

Unlike other touch up options that let you apply changes to parts of pictures, despeckling a photo makes global changes to the entire photo. It smoothes color transitions in an image, which can help remove the graininess that you sometimes see when you scan items from newspapers or magazines. Be careful, though, because despeckling too much can make items in an image indistinct.

TIP

Use Despeckle carefully.
Despeckling is a powerful option. Drag the Despeckle Amount slider one increment at a time until the image looks right. Use Undo if you go a step too far.

Despeckle

1. Click the photo.

2. Click Touch Up on the visual menu.

3. Click Despeckle on the Touch Up menu.

4. Drag the Despeckle Amount slider one increment to the right.

5. Repeat until you are satisfied with the image.

Despeckled image

10

Applying Effects

The fun of Microsoft PhotoDraw is how easily you can totally remake objects just by trying different menu options. With only a few clicks, you can give shadows to objects, make them transparent, or have them fade out or blend into other objects. It's just as easy to distort shapes (and the people in photos) into totally unreal figures.

But the most dazzling results come from the 3-D and designer effects that can transform flat shapes into three-dimensional objects and that can turn ordinary photos into museum-quality masterpieces. Try Wild Cave Painting or Glowing Edges on your favorite family snapshot. Just don't tell anyone that the sensational effect they're seeing took only a single click in PhotoDraw.

Adding a Shadow

Three-dimensional objects in the real world almost always cast shadows, so adding a shadow to an object, even a flat shape, in Photo-Draw can add realism and depth. PhotoDraw provides a gallery of shadow directions and lets you change the shadow transparency to let more of the background show through. You can also modify the softness of the shadow to give the impression of more diffuse lighting.

TIP

Removing a shadow. *After you attach a shadow to an object, the shadow remains with the object unless you select the object and select No Shadow in the gallery on the Shadow workpane.*

Add a Shadow

1. Click the object.

2. Click Effects on the visual menu.

3. Click Shadow on the Effects menu.

4. Click a shadow direction in the gallery.

5. Click the Color drop-down arrow to choose a different color for the shadow, if you want.

6. Drag the Transparency slider to the right to increase the amount of transparency in the shadow.

7. Drag the Soften slider to the right to make the edges of the shadow less distinct.

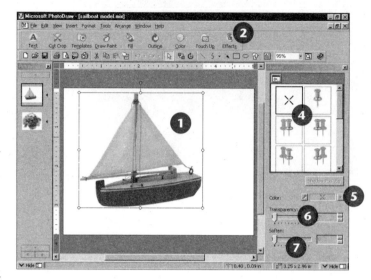

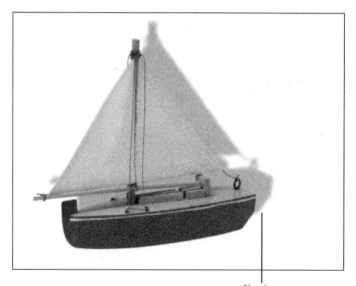

Shadow

Change the Shadow Position

1. Click the object that has the shadow.

2. Click Effects on the visual menu.

3. Click Shadow on the Effects menu.

4. Click the Shadow Position button.

5. Drag the shadow to change its position, or drag the handles on the shadow object to change the shadow's shape.

6. Click Finish.

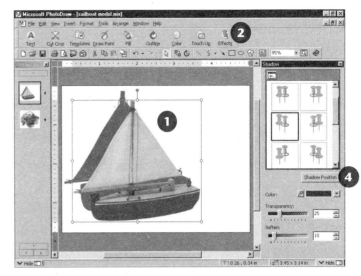

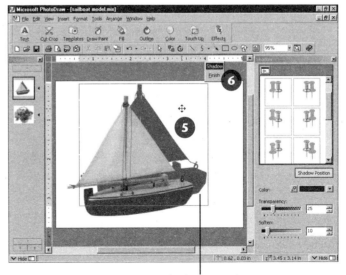

Shadow moved

Adding Transparency

By default, objects that you add to pictures are opaque; they cover up the objects that they overlap. But you can add transparency to an object so that objects that are underneath show through.

TIP

Transparency does not affect shadows. *Changing the transparency level of an object does not change the transparency of the shadow that you have added to the object. Shadows have their own transparency that you set separately.*

TIP

Use Fade Out to make objects become transparent. *When you add transparency with this procedure, the transparency is uniform across the object. To make the transparency change across an object, apply a fade-out effect instead. Giving a fade to a picture is covered on the opposite page.*

Set a Transparency Level

1. Click the object.

2. Click Effects on the visual menu.

3. Click Transparency on the Effects menu.

4. Drag the Transparency slider to the right to add transparency to the object.

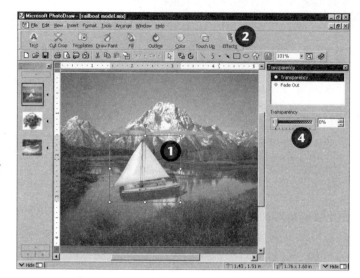

Semi-transparent object

Giving a Fade to a Picture

Applying the fade out effect to an object causes it appear to fade from top to bottom, left to right, or in any other direction that you choose. You can use the fade out effect to fade one photo into another in a montage or to fade an image into the background.

TIP

Making a cameo. *To achieve a cameo-like effect, choose the Radial shape for the Fade Out effect, and set Start to 0% transparency and End to 100% transparency.*

TIP

Removing a Fade-out. *To remove a fade-out effect, set the Start and End sliders to 0% transparency.*

Add a Fade-out

1. Click the object that you want to fade.

2. Click Effects on the Visual menu toolbar, and then click Fade Out on the Effects menu.

3. Drag the Start and End sliders to set transparency levels on one side of the photo and on the other.

4. Click the Expand Gallery button next to Shape and click a shape for the Fade Out effect.

5. Enter a new value in the Angle box if you want to change the angle at which the fade-out crosses the photo.

6. Drag the Center slider right or left to change how quickly the fade-out begins across the photo.

Fade-out effect

Adding a Distort Effect

Adding a distort effect lets you deform, warp, and twist images into a variety of pre-set shapes, from a funhouse bulge to a down-the-drain twirl. After you choose a distort type, you can change its amount and frequency to change the degree of the distortion.

PhotoDraw also lets you paint distortions on images by smearing, bulging, and shrinking whatever items that you click or drag across with the mouse pointer.

Choose a Distortion Type and Level

1 Click the object that you want to distort.

2 Click Effects on the visual menu.

3 Click Distort on the Effects menu.

4 Click a distort type in the gallery.

5 Click Settings in the workpane list to see additional options for the effect.

6 Drag the slider on the workpane to change the settings for the current effect.

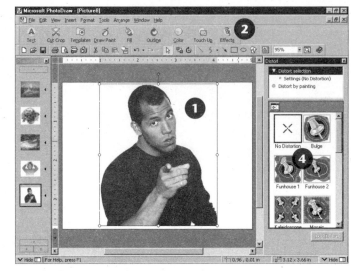

Using shrink on self-portraits. *Shrink is a useful distortion effect for self-portraits that show waistlines.*

Paint a Distortion onto a Picture

1. Click the object that you want to distort.

2. Click Effects on the visual menu.

3. Click Distort on the Effects menu.

4. Click Distort By Painting in the workpane list.

5. Click the drop-down arrow next to the Distortion box and click a distortion type in the list.

6. Click the Expand Gallery button next to Brush and choose a brush size.

7. Click the photo if you have chosen Shrink or Bulge. Drag across the photo if you have chosen Smear.

8. Click Undo Last to remove your last distortion or click Finish to finish.

Shrink

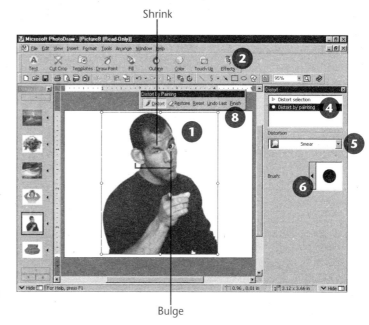

Bulge

10

Adding a 3-D Effect

PhotoDraw's designer 3-D effects raise flat shapes and give them sides and bevels (carved edges) so they take on a three-dimensional appearance. After you choose a designer 3-D effect for a shape, you can add a shadow or fill its face, bevel, or side with a color, gradient, texture, or photo.

TIP

3-D text. *You can create great looking 3-D text by applying a designer 3-D effect to a text object.*

SEE ALSO

For more information about creating 3-D text, see "Making Text 3-D" on page 60.

Choose a Designer 3-D Effect from the Gallery

1. Click a text object or an object that you have drawn or painted.

2. Click Effects on the visual menu.

3. Click 3-D on the Effects menu.

4. Click a designer 3-D Effect in the gallery.

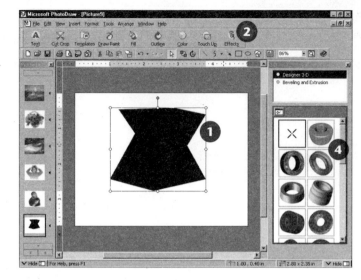

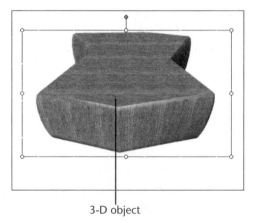

3-D object

Change the Fill of a 3-D Object

1. Click an object to which you applied a designer 3-D effect.

2. Click Fill in the workpane list.

3. Click one of the three Placement buttons to determine whether you are changing the fill of the face, the bevel, or the side.

4. Click the drop-down arrow next to the fill type box and choose Solid Color, Texture, Designer Gradient, Two-Color Gradient, or Picture.

5. Use the options on the workpane to fine-tune the appearance of the fill type that you have chosen.

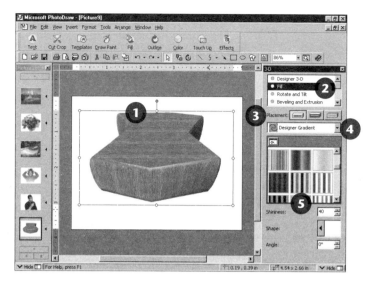

10

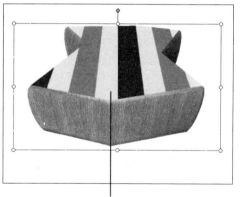

3-D object with designer gradient fill

Customizing the 3-D Effect

Even though each designer 3-D effect provides a preset rotation and tilt, the options on the 3-D workpane let you change the angle of the 3-D object by changing the rotation and tilt angles. You can also change how the edges of an object are carved by selecting a bevel style and changing the width and depth of the bevel. Changing the extrusion of a 3-D object changes its depth. Each designer 3-D effect supplies a preset extrusion depth.

TIP

Rotating by dragging.
You can also drag the rotation handle of a 3-D object to rotate it.

Change the 3-D Rotation and Tilt

① Click the 3-D object.

② Click Effects on the visual menu.

③ Click 3-D on the Effects menu.

④ Click Rotate And Tilt in the workpane list.

⑤ Click the arrows or enter numbers into the three rotation and tilt boxes.

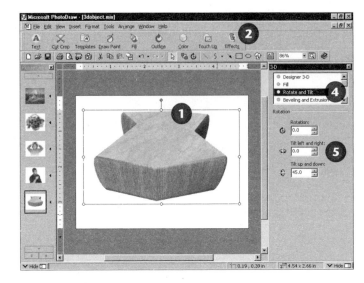

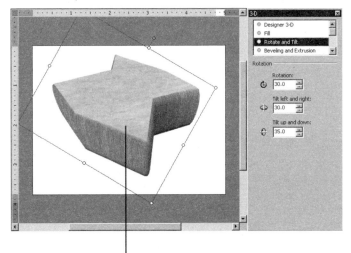

3-D object has been rotated and tilted.

Seeing the bevel better.
*To see a bevel more clearly,
enter large amounts for the
bevel depth and width and then
reduce the amounts until you
get the bevel you want.*

Alter the 3-D Bevel and Extrusion

1. Click the 3-D object.

2. Click Effects on the visual menu.

3. Click 3-D on the Effects menu.

4. Click Beveling And Extrusion in the workpane list.

5. Click the Expand Gallery button and click a bevel style.

6. Enter a new depth and width for the bevel.

7. Enter a new depth for the extrusion.

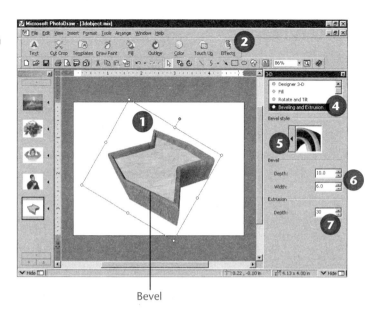

Bevel

10

Fine-Tuning the Lighting in the 3-D Effect

PhotoDraw's preset lighting options for 3-D objects shine light of different colors from different directions.

You can fine-tune the lighting option by choosing the color and position of three lights shining on the object, and setting a color for the ambient light that surrounds the object.

TIP

Changing your perspective. *The Perspective option on the lighting settings workpane lets you set whether the 3-D effect is relatively flat (with little perspective distortion) or quite deep (with lots of perspective distortion).*

TIP

Turning out a light. *To turn off a light, set its color to black.*

Change the Lighting

1. Click the 3-D object.

2. Click Effects on the visual menu.

3. Click 3-D on the Effects menu.

4. Click Lighting in the workpane list.

5. Click a preset lighting style in the gallery or click Settings for more options.

6. If you click Settings, click a light button labeled 1, 2, or 3 and then choose a color for the light. You can also change the tilt of each light by entering angles into the two Tilt boxes.

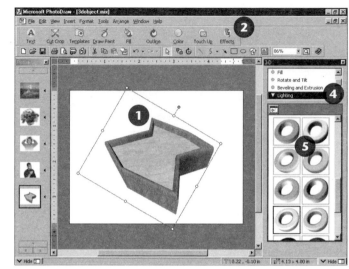

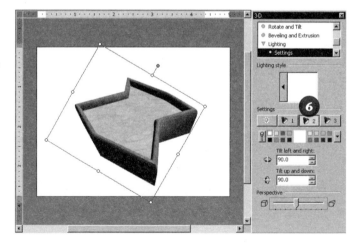

Putting a Photo on the Surface of a 3-D Object

After you apply a designer 3-D effect to a basic shape, you can put your favorite photo on the surface of the object (called the "face"). To accomplish this, choose Picture as the fill type, but rather than choosing one of the photos on the gallery, select a photo of your own.

TRY THIS

Using a 3-D object as a picture frame. *Fill a rectangular object with a texture, and then apply a Designer 3-D effect. Set the extrusion depth and then set the rotation and tilt values to 0. Fill the face of the object with a photo. The bevel creates an interesting picture frame.*

Fill a 3-D Object with a Photo

1. Select the 3-D object.

2. Click Effects on the visual menu.

3. Click 3-D on the Effects menu.

4. Click Fill in the workpane list.

5. Click the Face button.

6. Choose Picture from the fill type list.

7. Click Browse.

8. Choose the photo with which to fill the face of the 3-D object.

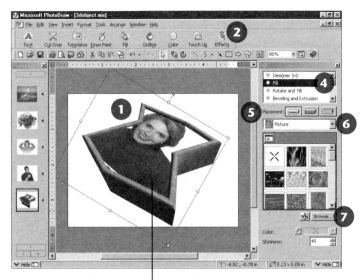

Photo on face of 3-D object

10

Adding a Designer Effect

Designer effects transform images that you've assembled and photos that you've scanned into works of art. PhotoDraw provides more than a hundred different artistic effects in the gallery.

Each effect has a preset group of options, but you can experiment with different settings on the workpane and create infinite varieties of effects. For example, the Rough Pastels effect has dozens of textures from which you can choose.

TIP

Filtering the gallery. *Photo-Draw provides so many effects that you may want to filter the display of effects in the gallery by choosing a type from the type list on the workpane.*

Choose an Effect

1. Click the object.

2. Click Effects on the visual menu.

3. Click Designer Effect on the Effects menu.

4. Click an effect in the gallery.

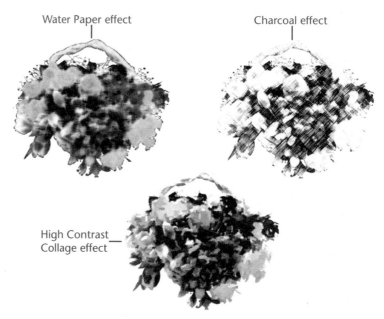

Water Paper effect

Charcoal effect

High Contrast Collage effect

Layering effects. *To layer effects on top of each other, apply an effect and then click Lock Effect on the Designer Effects workpane. The next effect will then add to the previous effect rather than replace it.*

Creating interesting backgrounds. *You can cut out a small portion of a photo or draw and paint a random pattern of shapes and then experiment with various designer effects until you have achieved an interesting and colorful texture that you can use for the background of a Web page or presentation.*

Change the Settings for the Effect

1. Choose a designer effect for an object.

2. Click Settings in the workpane list.

3. Use the options that appear on the workpane to change different aspects of the effect.

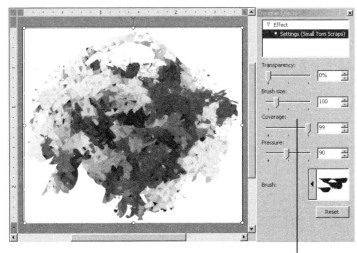

Options for Small Torn Scraps effect

10

Combining Images

Until now, the procedures in this book have focused on things you can do with individual objects. You've learned to edit objects, change their color, touch up photo objects, and create and customize text objects.

In this section, you learn to take advantage of another of Microsoft PhotoDraw's key features: its ability to let you easily copy objects from various pictures into new arrangements or compositions. This unparalleled freedom to mix and match elements and create new pictures from existing objects makes it easy to create complex graphics from simple components and to assemble sophisticated pictures from pre-existing elements.

Opening a Picture's Object List

When a picture is composed of multiple objects, you can open the picture's object list to see a visual listing of the objects. After the list is open, you can drag objects from the list onto other pictures, rearrange the *stacking order* of the objects (their relative positions on top of each other), and delete objects.

SEE ALSO

For more information about the parts of the PhotoDraw screen, see "The PhotoDraw Screen" on page 10.

Show the Object List for a Picture

1. Open a picture composed of multiple objects.

2. In the picture list, click the left arrow button to the right of the picture.

3. If the object list is long, use the single arrow buttons at the top and bottom of the list to scroll through the list. Use the double arrow buttons to scroll farther.

4. Click the right arrow button to close the list after you are finished with it.

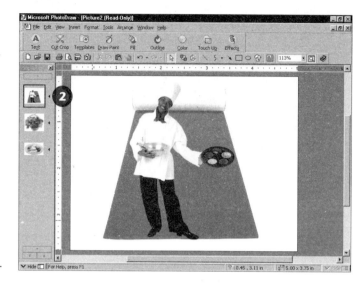

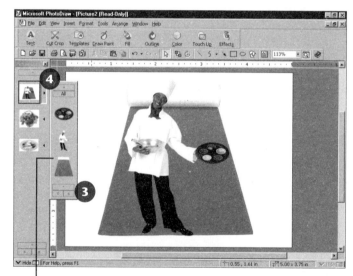

Object list

Selecting Objects with the Object List

You can select objects by clicking them in a picture, but sometimes pictures are composed of many overlapping objects and it can be difficult to select just one. That's when you should turn to the picture's object list, which lays out all of a picture's objects in a neatly organized column.

TIP

Browsing through a picture's objects. *To scan through the objects in a picture, pass the mouse pointer over each object in the object list. As the mouse pointer passes over an object in the object list, the object in the list and the object in the picture are surrounded by a black selection box.*

Select an Object in the Object List

1. In the picture list, click the left arrow button next to a picture to open its object list.

2. Click an object in the object list to select it.

Selected object

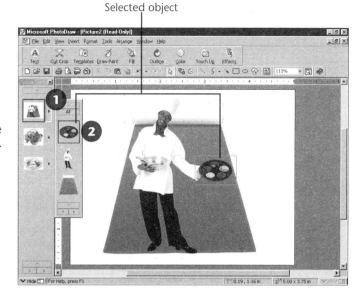

Dragging an Image or Text from an Object List

Not only can you view the objects in a picture by opening its object list, but you can also drag an object from the object list into another picture that is open on the work area. This copies the object into the picture.

TIP

Dragging objects copies them. *Dragging an object from an object list into another picture copies the object. The object is not moved, so the original remains in the object list where it came from.*

Drag an Object to a Picture

1. Open two pictures, one that is the source for the object you want to copy, and the other that is the destination.

2. In the picture list, click the destination picture (the picture to which you will drag the object).

3. Open the object list of the source picture (the picture from which you will drag the object).

4. Drag the object from the object list into the picture in the work area.

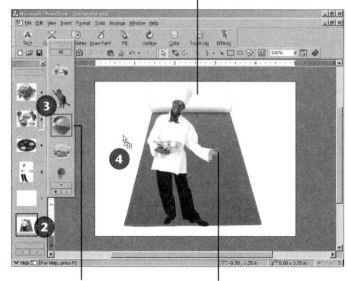

Destination picture

Drag object from here...   ...to here.

Object dragged into picture

Inserting an Object from a File

You can insert an object from a file on your hard disk to add it to the picture and to the picture's object list.

To add the object to the picture list but not to the open picture, you must open rather than insert it. The object appears in the picture list and you can then drag it into other pictures.

SEE ALSO

For information about opening a file, see "Opening Something Old" on page 12.

TIP

Previewing items. *To preview the items in the Insert dialog box, click the Preview button on the toolbar in the dialog box.*

Preview

Insert from a File

1. Open the picture into which you want to insert an object from a file.

2. Click From File on the Insert menu.

3. In the Look In list, click the folder that contains the object.

4. Click the filename of the object you want to insert.

5. Click Open to insert the object at the center of the current picture.

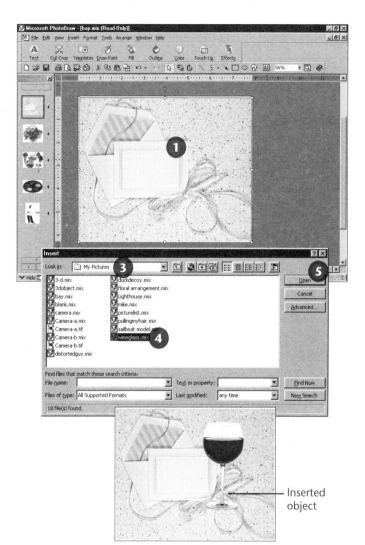

Inserted object

Visually Inserting an Object from a File

If you know the filename of the object you want to insert, you can click From File on the Insert menu. But if you want to browse through the images on your hard disk or on a CD-ROM, you can use Visual Insert, which shows thumbnail versions of the images in a folder. You can click a thumbnail to select an image, and then insert it into the current picture.

Visually Insert from a File

1. Open the picture into which you want to insert an object from a file.

2. Click Visual Insert on the Insert menu.

3. In the two lists under Look In, click the disk and folder that you want to browse.

4. Click the thumbnail of the image to insert.

5. Click Insert.

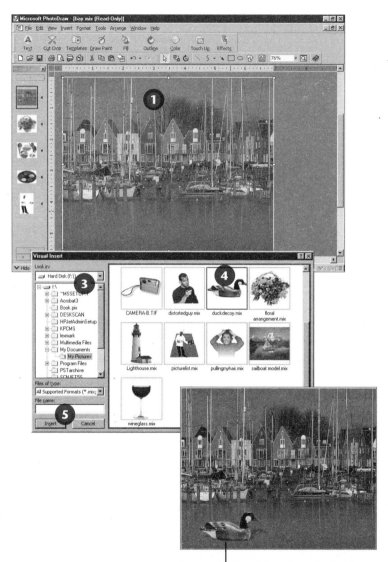

Inserted object (also given shadow)

Deleting an Object

When you delete an object from a picture, it is removed from the picture and from the picture's object list. The object is not deleted from your hard disk, though, so you can use it later in another picture.

TIP

Shortcut. *You can also click an object in a picture and press the Delete key to remove it from a picture's object list.*

Delete an Object

1. Click the picture in the picture list.

2. Click the left arrow button next to the picture to open the picture's object list.

3. Click the object that you want to delete in the object list.

4. Press the Delete key.

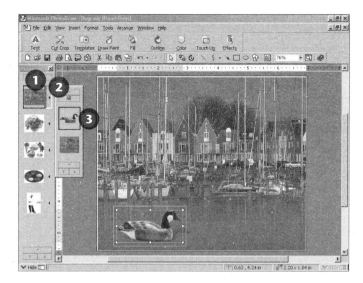

Object has been deleted.

Swapping Objects

You can drag any object from a picture into the picture list. Then you can save the object from the picture list in its own file.

You can also replace an object in one picture with an object from a different picture's object list.

TIP

Preserving customized objects. *If you've spent time customizing an object by editing it, you should drag it to the picture list so you can save it in its own PhotoDraw file.*

TIP

Objects from the work area. *You can keep objects that you might want to use open on the work area, and then zoom out and replace objects in the picture with them.*

Move an Object to the Picture List

1. Click an object in a picture or in a picture's object list.

2. Drag the object from the picture into the picture list, below the last picture in the list.

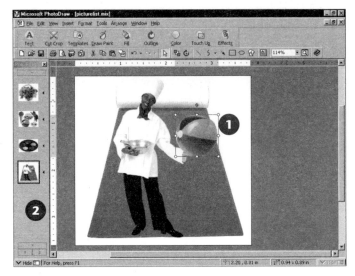

Object in its own picture in the picture list

Replacements get the same attributes. *When you replace an object, the attributes of the original object, such as its shadowing and transparency, are given to the replacement object. You can use this to transfer attributes between objects. Just make sure that you retain a copy of the original object if you want to keep it.*

Replace an Object with a Picture List Object

1. Click an object in a picture or in a picture's object list.

2. Click the Replace button on the toolbar.

3. Click an object in a different picture's object list.

Replace button

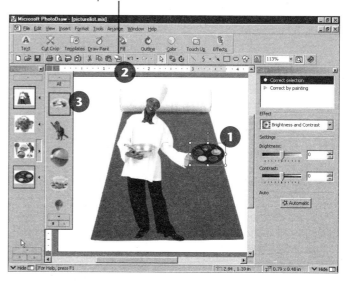

Replacement object

11

Restacking Objects

With the order options, you can move the objects in a picture in front of (Bring Forward) or behind (Send Backward) other objects in the picture to change how they overlap. You can also send an object to the top of the stack (Bring To Front) or to the bottom (Send To Back). You can use these features to move an object from the background to the front while you work on it and then send it back to the background.

> **TIP**
>
> **Using the object list.** *You can also drag an object up or down the object list to move it forward or backward.*

> **TIP**
>
> **Order on the shortcut menu.** *You can click an object with the right mouse button and choose an order option from the shortcut menu.*

Restack Objects

1. Click the object that you want to move forward or backward.

2. Click the Order button on the toolbar.

3. Click an order option on the drop-down menu.

Order button

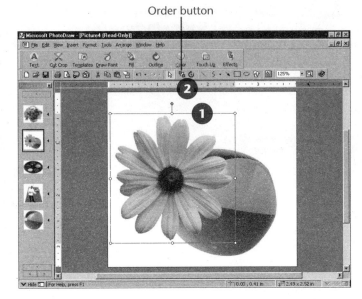

Object has been sent backward.

Grouping Objects

You can temporarily combine objects into a single object by grouping them. You can then modify the group with all the techniques that you'd use to edit each object. When you group objects, they have a single set of handles. When you ungroup them, each object retains the changes you made to the group, such as a color adjustment that you've made.

SEE ALSO

For information about editing objects, see Section 7, "Editing Individual Objects."

Group and Ungroup Objects

1. Hold down the Shift key and click multiple objects in a picture or in a picture's object list.

2. Click Group on the Arrange menu.

3. To ungroup the objects, click the group and click Ungroup on the Arrange menu.

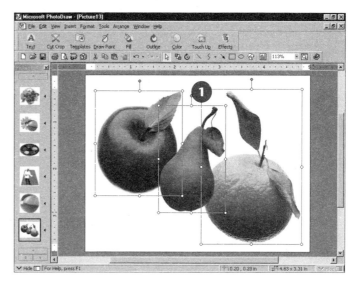

Grouped objects

11

Aligning Objects

By aligning objects, you can line up their edges or their centers. You can eyeball objects into position, dragging them into alignment, but you can align objects much more precisely with the Align command.

In addition to aligning multiple objects with each other, you can align one or more objects in relation to the picture area. For example, you can center an object at the center of a picture.

TIP

How objects align. *When you align the tops of two objects, they line up with the object closest to the top of the picture. When you align their right edges, they align with the rightmost object, and so on.*

Align Objects with Each Other

1. Hold down the Shift key and click multiple objects in a picture or in a picture's object list.

2. Point to Align on the Arrange menu.

3. If the Relative To Picture Area option on the Align menu is turned on (pressed in), click it to turn it off.

4. Point to Align again on the Arrange menu.

5. Click one of the six Align options on the Align menu.

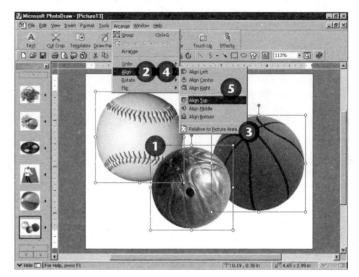

Top-aligned objects

Deselecting objects. *After you align multiple objects, you can click Select None on the Edit menu to deselect all the objects.*

Corner aligning. *To align an object with the corner of a picture, first align it with one side, and then align it with the adjacent side.*

Align Objects with the Picture Area

1 Select one or more objects.

2 Point to Align on the Arrange menu.

3 Click Relative To Picture Area on the Align menu if it is not already turned on.

4 Point to Align on the Arrange menu again.

5 Click one of the six Align options on the Align menu.

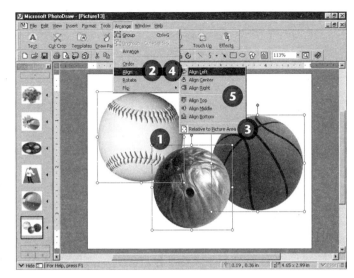

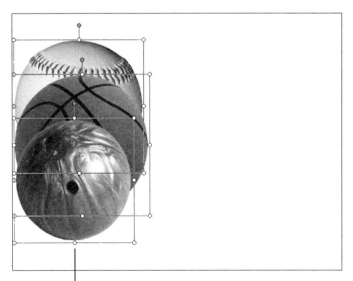

Objects are left-aligned with picture area.

Closing Pictures

When you finish working with a picture in the picture list, you can close it. Closing a picture does not delete it from your hard disk. It just removes it from the Photo-Draw window and from the picture list.

If you try to close a picture that you have not saved or that you have changed, PhotoDraw asks whether you want to save it. Click Yes to save the picture, click No to close the picture without saving it, and click Cancel to stop trying to close the picture.

> **TIP**
>
> **Quick closure.** *You can also click a picture in the picture list with the right mouse button and click Close from the shortcut menu.*

Close a Picture

1. Click a picture in the picture list.

2. Click Close on the File menu.

The second picture in the picture list is closed and the first picture becomes the visible picture in the work area.

12

Creating Pictures from Templates

Templates are perfect for people who are not trained artists, but who still want professional results. Created by artists, templates provide polished designs for hundreds of different Web page graphics, like buttons and banners, and business and home-related projects, such as flyers, labels, invitations, and postcards. The designs range from formal to festive so you are certain to find a look that suits you. After you choose a template, you need only replace the sample text and photos with your own to achieve a finished, professional look.

Choosing a Template Category and Style

The first step in using a - template to start a Photo-Draw project is to choose a template from the hundreds that are available to you. PhotoDraw provides five types of templates, a handful of categories for each type, and a dozen or more template styles in each category. You need to select a template type, choose a category, and then pick a style to get the one you want.

TIP

Customizing templates.
You cannot modify PhotoDraw's collection of templates or add your own to those that appear when you choose Design Template, but you can open a template and then save it in a file on your hard disk. Then you can customize this file and use it to start new PhotoDraw projects.

Open a Template When You Start PhotoDraw

1. Start PhotoDraw.

2. Click Design Template.

3. Click OK.

4. Insert the second PhotoDraw CD when prompted.

5. On the Templates workpane, click the down-arrow next to the Gallery Type list.

6. Click a Template category in the Gallery Type list.

7. Click a category in the gallery.

8. Double-click a template style.

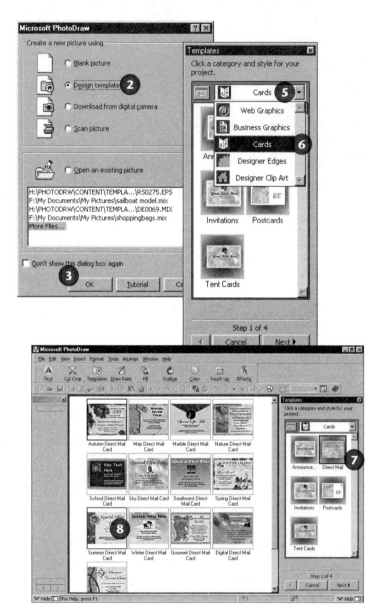

Trying a different template.
If you open a template but decide that you'd rather try a different template style, you can click the left arrow button at the bottom of the Templates work-pane to return to the display of template styles.

Buttons and banners for Microsoft FrontPage. *Some of the Web page–related templates in PhotoDraw are meant to complement the Web site designs in Microsoft FrontPage.*

Downloading additional templates. *You can download additional templates for Photo-Draw from the Microsoft Web site at http://officeupdate. microsoft.com/default.htm.*

Open a Template When PhotoDraw Is Already Running

1. Click Templates on the visual menu.

2. Click a template type on the Templates menu.

3. Insert the second PhotoDraw CD when prompted.

4. Click a category in the gallery.

5. Double-click a template style.

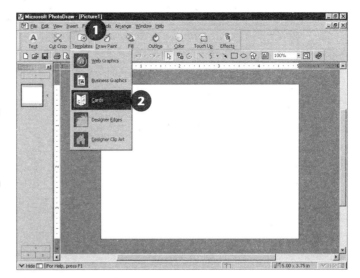

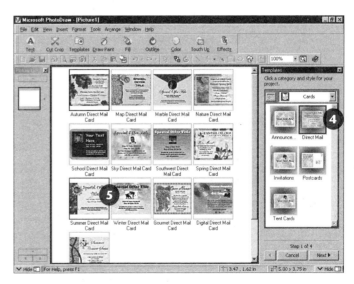

12

About Templates

Templates are ready-made designs you can use for Web pages, business graphics, and mailers, such as invitations and postcards. When you select a template, you get a complete but generic project that has sample text, graphics, and photos arranged in a professional design. To convert the generic template into something more suited to your needs, you simply replace the generic elements in the template with text, graphics, and photos of your own. The result looks similar to the original design, but it includes your information rather than the generic samples.

The three types of templates are shown in the table at the right: Web Graphics, Business Graphics, and Cards. Each type offers a number of categories. Each category, in turn, includes a dozen or more styles, so you have many, many generic designs to use as the basis for your own, personal projects.

On the Templates menu, you'll also find two additional options: Designer Edges and Designer Clip Art. Designer edges are a wide collection of patterns, styles, and shapes for the borders of photos. The collection shows dozens of sample photos that have had their edges customized. You can choose one of these samples and use its edge by replacing the generic photo with your own.

Designer clip art contains a resource of hundreds of useful illustrations. After you select an illustration that's appropriate for your needs, you can choose any of Photo-Draw's artistic or photo brushes with which to draw it to give it the look you want.

Sample certificate template

Sample postcard template

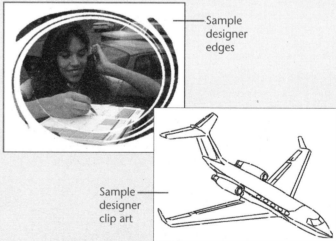

Sample designer edges

Sample designer clip art

WEB GRAPHICS

Banners

Circular Buttons

Connecting Buttons

Festive Buttons

Rectangular Buttons

BUSINESS GRAPHICS

Bulletins

Certificates

Flyers

Icons

Labels–Decorative

Labels–Return Address

Labels–Round

Logos

CARDS

Announcements

Direct Mail

Invitations

Postcards

Tent Cards

12

Replacing Images

Most templates have at least one image in the background, if not a photo in the foreground. You can select these sample images or photos and replace them with your own. Your photo then appears in the same position and at the same size as the sample photo.

TIP

Moving the image object. *The position of images in templates is not fixed. You can move them or resize them by dragging their handles, just as you do with any object in a picture.*

SEE ALSO

For more information about opening a template, see "Choosing a Template Category and Style" on page 142.

Replace an Image Object with a Picture List Object

1. Open the picture that contains the image object that you want to use as a replacement for the sample on the template.

2. Open a template.

3. In the picture list, click the arrow next to the picture that contains the replacement object to open the picture's object list.

4. On the template, click the image object that you want to replace.

5. Click the Replace button.

6. Click the replacement object in the opened object list.

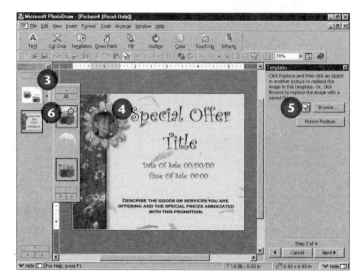

Replacement object in place

The Picture Position button. *When you replace a sample with your own photo, your photo is reduced or enlarged to fit the space of the original image. To select the photo and resize or reposition it within that space, click the Picture Position button, and then drag the handles that appear around the photo.*

For more information about opening a template, see "Choosing a Template Category and Style" on page 142.

Replace an Image Object with a Picture from a File

1. Open a template.

2. Click an image object on the template.

3. Click the Browse button.

4. Click the disk and folder in the Look In list that contains the replacement graphic.

5. Click the thumbnail of the replacement graphic.

6. Click Open.

7. Click Next on the Templates workpane.

Replacing Text

You can enter your own text in place of the sample text on the template. The text that you enter is styled like the sample text, but you can easily change the font, font size, and font style.

TIP

Breaking a line. *To end a line and start a new one, click in the text at the place you want the line break to occur and press Shift+Enter.*

SEE ALSO

For more information about opening a template, see "Choosing a Template Category and Style" on page 142.

Replace a Text Object

1. Open a template.

2. Click the text object that you want to replace.

3. Type new text in place of the existing text on the Templates workpane.

4. Change the Font, Size, and Style options on the Templates workpane to change the appearance of the text, if you want.

5. Click another text object and repeat steps 3 and 4 to continue changing the template, if you want.

6. Click Next.

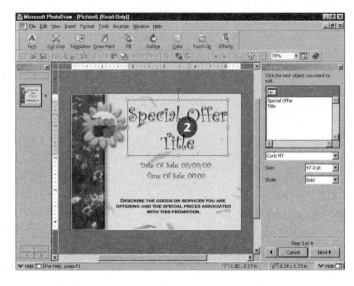

Saving the Picture

After you customize a template with your own text, graphics, and photos, you are ready to save it. PhotoDraw reminds you to save your work with a message in the Templates workpane.

SEE ALSO

For more information about opening a template, see "Choosing a Template Category and Style" on page 142.

SEE ALSO

For more information about replacing text and photos in a template, see "Replacing Images" on page 146 and "Replacing Text" on page 148.

SEE ALSO

For more information about saving files in PhotoDraw, see "Saving a Picture" on page 180.

Save the Picture

1. Open a template and replace the text and images with your own.

2. When the Click Finish To Complete Your Project message appears on the Templates workpane, click Finish.

3. Click Save As or Save For Use In on the File menu.

4. If you clicked Save As, enter a name for the picture and click Save. If you clicked Save For Use In, follow the steps of the Save For Use In Wizard and click Save at the last step.

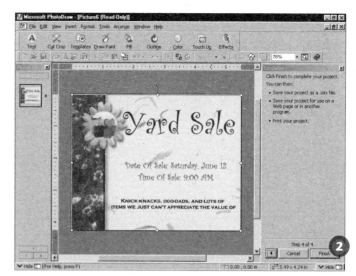

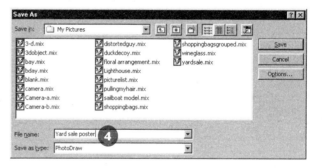

12

Using a Designer Edge

Unlike other templates, designer edges do not offer complete project designs. Instead, they give stylized borders to your plain, rectangular photos that have straight edges. These borders look soft, brushed, textured, shaped, or beveled, among many possibilities. You can then use these photos, with their unique designer edges, in other projects.

Sample designer edges

Painted Circle Edge   Horizontal Brush Strokes Edge   Pointed Circular Edge

Watchband Edge   Smudged Edge   Musical Notes Edge

Flower Petal Edge   Spotted Edge   Tacks Edge

Use a Designer Edge

1. Click Templates on the visual menu.

2. Click Designer Edges on the Templates menu.

3. Click a category in the gallery: Artistic, Paper, or Traditional.

4. Click a designer edge style.

5. Click Next.

6. Click Browse and choose your own photo, or if the photo you want is already open in the picture list, click the Replace button and then click the photo in the picture list.

7. Click Next.

8. Click Finish to close the Templates workpane.

Replaced photo

Using a Designer Clip Art Selection

A designer clip art selection is unlike most clips from the clip gallery because it is a drawing composed of lines rather than a photograph or an image composed of shapes. After you select a designer clip art selection, you can choose the brush with which to draw its lines. A plain brush, an artistic brush, or a photographic brush will give the clip art very different looks.

Use a Designer Clip Art Selection

1. Click Templates on the visual menu.

2. Click Designer Clip Art on the Templates menu.

3. Click a category in the gallery.

4. Click a clip art selection.

5. Click Next.

6. Choose Plain, Artistic Brushes, or Photo Brushes from the workpane drop-down list.

7. Click a brush style in the gallery and choose a color in the gallery.

8. Drag the Width slider to the right to make the lines in the clip art selection wider.

9. Click Next and then click Finish on the workpane at the next step.

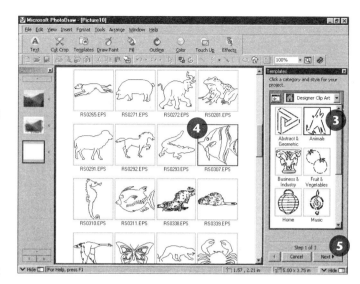

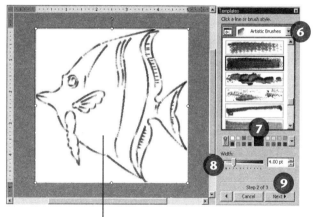

Designer clip art selection drawn with the Oil–Heavy Wide artistic brush.

13

Drawing and Painting

Although much of Microsoft PhotoDraw's focus is on working with photographic images, its drawing and painting tools are surprisingly powerful.

For starters, you get a basic palette of simple, geometric shapes with which to draw, such as lines, rectangles, and circles. But you can also choose from a collection of more sophisticated shapes like stars, banners, and arrows. If you've got the talent, you can even create your own works of art with PhotoDraw's artistic and photo paintbrushes.

When you combine PhotoDraw's drawing and painting tools with its options for filling and outlining shapes, and then top that off with effects like shadows and designer effects, you've got some pretty powerful tools at your disposal.

153

Adding Lines

Lines are the simplest shapes to draw. One point marks their start and a second marks their end. PhotoDraw's artistic and photo brushes give you almost unlimited possibilities for their appearance.

TIP

Constraining a line. *To constrain the line you are drawing so it is exactly horizontal, vertical, or diagonal, press and hold down the Shift key while you draw the line.*

TIP

Graphic lines for Web pages. *PhotoDraw's artistic and photo brushes let you create graphic lines that are ideal for separating areas on Web pages.*

Draw a Line

1. Click the Line button.

2. Click a line style in the gallery.

3. Click a color chip to choose a color for the line.

4. Drag the Width slider to the right to increase the width of the line or click the up or down arrows next to the current size to change the width in quarter-point increments.

5. Position the mouse pointer on the picture at the starting point for the line.

6. Press and hold the mouse button down and drag the mouse to the ending point for the line.

7. Release the mouse button.

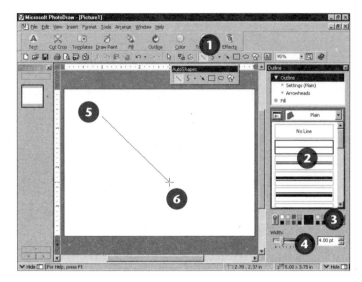

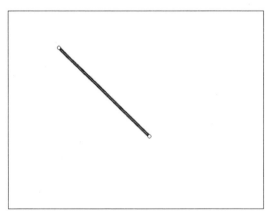

SEE ALSO

For more information about choosing colors for a line and the other objects you learn to draw in this section, see "Changing the Color of an Object" on page 86, and "Using Color Palettes" on page 90.

Draw a Line with an Artistic or Photo Brush

1. Click the Line button.

2. Put the mouse pointer at the start of the line, hold the mouse button, drag to the end, and release the mouse button.

3. Click the drop-down arrow next to the Gallery Type box.

4. Click Artistic Brushes or Photo Brushes in the Gallery Type list.

5. Click a brush style in the gallery and click a color chip to choose a brush color.

6. Drag the Width slider to the right to increase the width of the line.

7. If you want, try other photo or artistic brushes until you are satisfied with your choice.

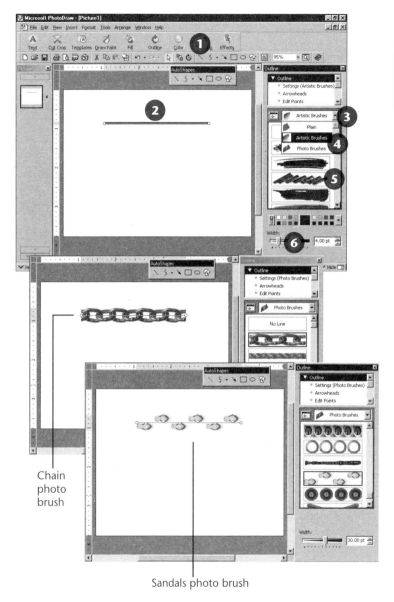

Chain photo brush

Sandals photo brush

Drawing Rectangles

The second easiest shape to draw is a rectangle. Like lines, only two points mark its shape by defining the opposite corners of the rectangle. Unlike lines, though, rectangles have fills so you can have fun with the interior space of a rectangle in addition to the outline of the rectangle.

TIP

Drawing a square. *Hold down the Shift key as you draw a rectangle to get a perfect square.*

TRY THIS

Use the visual menu. *The workpanes can be confusing, especially when you change from one option to another in the workpane list. Sometimes it's easier to use the Fill and Outline menus on the visual menu. When you make a choice on these menus, the workpane adjusts to show the appropriate options for your choice.*

Draw a Rectangle

1. Click the Rectangle button.

2. Place the mouse pointer at one corner of the rectangle, hold down the mouse button and drag to the opposite corner, and release the mouse button.

3. Click the drop-down arrow next to the Gallery Type box.

4. In the Gallery Type list, click a plain, artistic, or photo brush with which to create the outline of the rectangle.

5. Click options on the workpane for the brush you have chosen.

6. Click Fill in the workpane list.

7. Click fill type in the fill type list.

8. Choose options on the workpane for the fill type you have chosen.

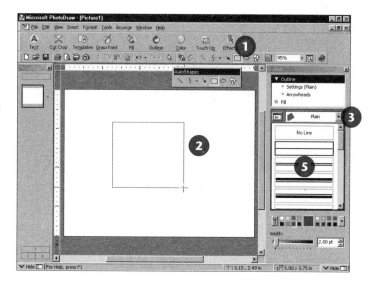

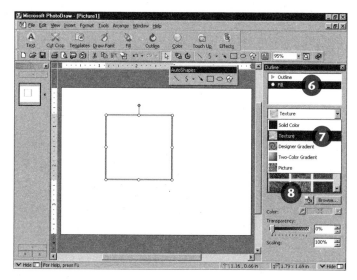

Drawing Curves

To draw a curve, you click points for PhotoDraw to connect with a smoothly flowing shape. The more points you click, the more control you gain over the shape of the curve.

Don't worry if the shape of the curve is not perfect. After you draw a curve, you can move its points to change its shape.

TIP

Another way to draw.
Although it's easy to start a curve by clicking the Curve button on the Standard toolbar, you can also click the Draw Paint button on the visual menu and then choose Draw from the Draw Paint menu.

SEE ALSO

For information about reshaping a curve, see "Moving a Point" on page 171.

Draw a Curve

1. Click the Curve button.

2. Click the first point of the curve.

3. Click additional points for the curve to pass through.

4. Double-click the last point.

5. Click the drop-down arrow next to the Gallery Type list.

6. Click an option in the Gallery Type list.

7. Use the options on the Outline workpane to change the appearance of the curve.

8. To change the fill, click Fill on the visual menu, and then choose an option on the Fill menu.

9. Adjust the options on the workpane for the choice you made on the Fill menu.

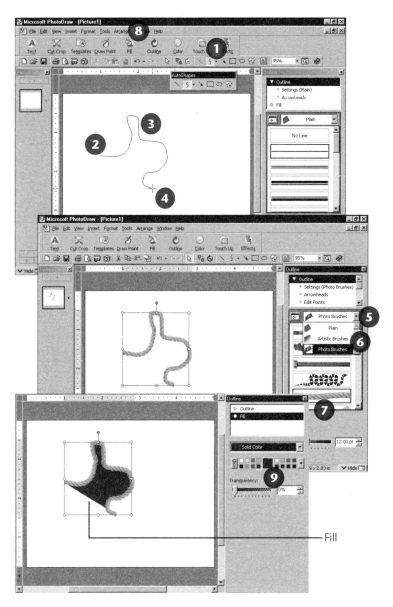

Fill

Making Freeforms

A freeform is a shape that is composed of a combination of straight-line segments and curved segments. To draw the straight-line segments, you click points. To draw the curved segments, you hold down the mouse button and drag the mouse pointer.

A freeform can be open so it has no fill, or closed. To close a freeform shape, click near the first point. The shape is closed and you can then change its fill.

TIP

Freeform vs. scribble.
A scribble is similar to a free-form, but it has no straight-line segments. Use a freeform when you need straight-line segments. Otherwise, just draw a scribble.

TIP

The Curve button. *The Curve button on the Standard toolbar displays the type of curved shape that you used last, so it may display a freeform or a scribble.*

Draw a Freeform Shape

1. Click the drop-down arrow next to the Curve button.

2. Click the Freeform button.

3. Alternate between dragging across the picture to draw the shape and clicking to add straight-line segments to the shape.

4. Double-click to finish the freeform.

5. Use the Fill and Outline menus on the visual menu and their corresponding work-panes to change the appearance of the shape.

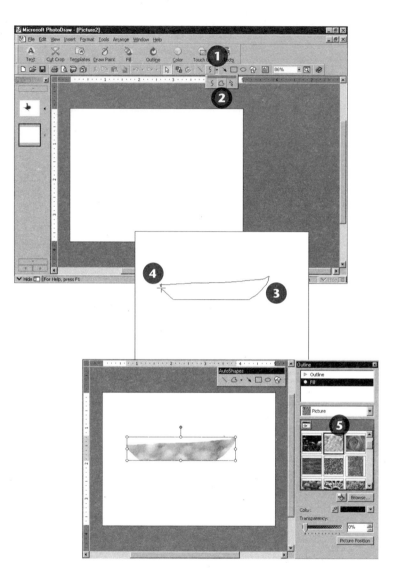

Scribbling

A scribble is just what it sounds like: a freeform shape that you draw by dragging across the screen. You can sign your favorite PhotoDraw artwork with a scribble.

Scribbles can be open or closed, depending on whether you return to the starting point when you finish the shape.

TIP

Oops. *If you release the mouse button by mistake while you are scribbling, you must undo the scribble and start a new one.*

TIP

Scribbles are autoshapes.
Scribbles, like the lines, curves, and arrows on the Standard toolbar, are autoshapes. You also find them on the menu that opens when you click the AutoShapes button on the Standard toolbar.

Draw a Scribble

1. Click the drop-down arrow next to the Curve button.

2. Click the Scribble button.

3. Hold down the mouse button and drag across the picture to scribble on it.

4. Release the mouse button to finish the scribble.

5. Use the Fill and Outline menus on the visual menu and their corresponding work-panes to change the appearance of the shape.

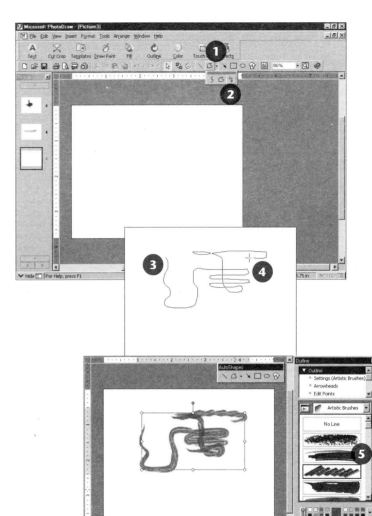

Pointing with Arrows

Arrows are lines with arrowheads at either or both ends. PhotoDraw gives you the choice to draw an arrow right off the bat or add an arrowhead to an existing line to achieve the same result.

Arrows can only be drawn with a plain brush. Lines drawn with artistic and photo brushes cannot have arrowheads.

TIP

Changing the arrowhead width independently. *After you draw an arrow, you can change the size of the line and arrowhead proportionately by clicking Settings in the workpane list and changing the width of the arrow. To change the arrowhead size without changing the line width, click Arrowheads in the workpane list and use the Size options.*

Draw an Arrow

1. Click the Arrow button.

2. Place the mouse pointer at the starting point for the arrow.

3. Drag the mouse pointer in the direction you want the arrow to point.

4. Release the mouse button to finish the arrow.

5. In the End area of the workpane, click the drop-down arrow next to the Style box and click one of the six arrow styles.

6. In the End area of the workpane, click the drop-down arrow next to the Size box and click one of the six arrowhead sizes.

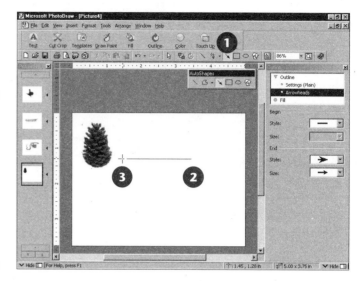

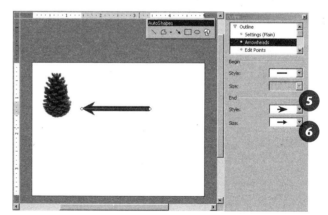

Begin and end. *No matter which way they point, arrows have specific beginnings and endings based on how they were drawn. The starting point of the original arrow is the* begin. *The ending point is the* end. *You'll see these two terms on the Outline workpane.*

Converting lines to arrows. *You can also add arrowheads to lines by using the Arrowheads option in the workpane list. Remember, though, that you can only add arrowheads to lines drawn with a plain brush.*

Change the Arrowhead

1. Click an arrow.

2. If the Outline workpane is not open, click Outline on the visual menu, and then click Plain on the Outline menu.

3. Click Arrowheads in the workpane list.

4. Click the drop-down arrow next to Style and choose a different arrowhead style for either the beginning or the ending of the line.

5. Click the drop-down arrow next to Size and choose a different arrowhead size for either the beginning or the ending of the line.

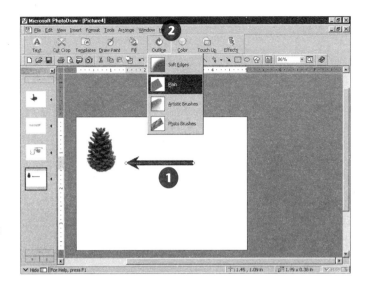

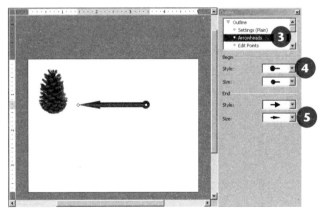

Making Ellipses

An ellipse (an oval or circle) is another basic shape in PhotoDraw's arsenal. Ellipses have outlines and fills, so you can use the Outline and Fill options on the visual menu to change their appearance.

TIP

Drawing a circle. *Hold down the Shift key as you draw an ellipse to get a perfect circle.*

Draw an Ellipse

1. Click the Ellipse button.

2. Position the mouse pointer at one corner of an imaginary rectangle that should roughly contain the ellipse.

3. Hold down the mouse button and drag across to the opposite corner of the rectangle.

4. Release the mouse button to create the ellipse.

5. Use the Fill and Outline menus on the visual menu and their corresponding workpanes to change the appearance of the ellipse.

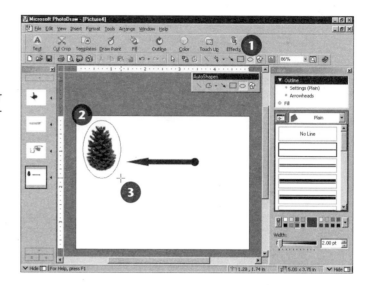

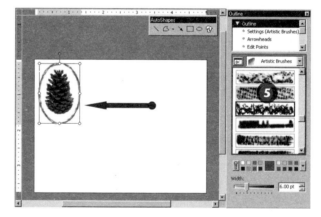

Placing an Autoshape

In this section, you've used the basic shapes that are displayed on the Standard toolbar, but PhotoDraw offers dozens more. These are available on the AutoShapes menu, which appears when you click the AutoShapes button on the Standard toolbar.

PhotoDraw's autoshapes include everything from simple shapes to arrows, flowchart symbols, stars and banners, and cartoon-type callouts (also known as *thought bubbles*).

Select and Draw an Autoshape

1 Click the AutoShapes button.

2 Point to an autoshapes category on the AutoShapes menu.

3 Click an autoshape.

4 Position the mouse pointer on the picture.

5 Hold down the mouse button and drag across the picture to create the autoshape.

6 Release the mouse button to complete the autoshape.

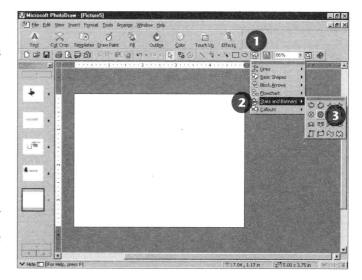

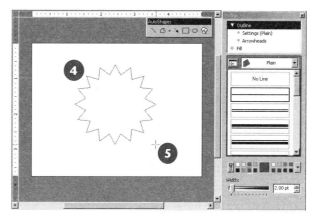

Reshaping Autoshapes

Many autoshapes have one or more small, yellow adjustment handles that you can drag to change the look of the autoshape's key feature. The smiley face autoshape has an adjustment handle that you can use to change the smile to a frown. Other autoshapes aren't as much fun to adjust. The adjustment handle on the 3-D cube changes the depth of the cube, for example.

Reshape an Autoshape

1 Click the autoshape.

2 Drag the adjustment handle left, right, up, or down until you see a change in the appearance of the autoshape.

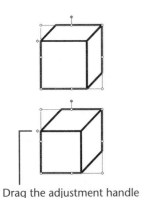

Drag the adjustment handle to change the depth of a cube.

Adjustment handle

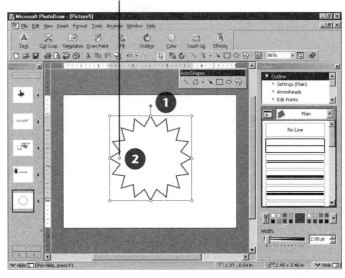

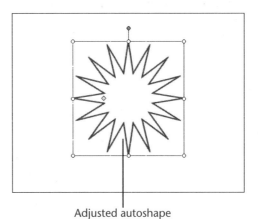

Adjusted autoshape

Painting in PhotoDraw

You paint in PhotoDraw the same way you draw scribbles, by dragging the mouse pointer across the picture using an artistic or photo brush. The difference is that a scribble can be reshaped with Edit Points (covered in the next section) while a painting stroke cannot.

TIP

Multiple strokes become a single object. *You can paint multiple strokes before clicking Finish. When you click Finish, the strokes become a single object.*

SEE ALSO

For more information about Edit Points mode, see "Entering and Exiting Edit Points Mode" on page 170.

Paint

1. Click the Draw Paint button on the visual menu.

2. Click Paint on the Draw Paint menu.

3. Click the drop-down arrow next to the Gallery Type list and click a brush type.

4. Click a brush style in the gallery.

5. Click a color chip to select a color.

6. Drag the Width slider to change the brush width.

7. Position the mouse pointer (a crosshair) on the picture and press and hold down the mouse button.

8. Drag the mouse pointer across the picture to paint a stroke and release the mouse button at the end of the stroke.

9. Click Undo Last to remove the last stroke or click Finish to finish painting.

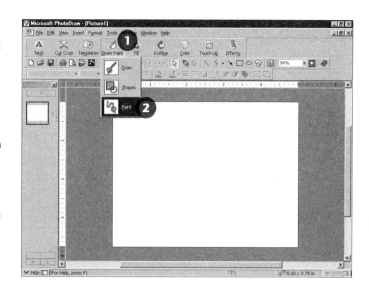

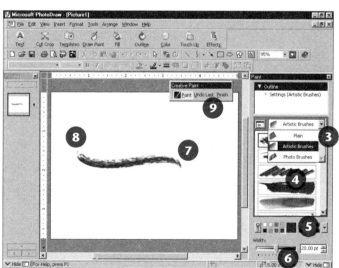

Modifying Painted Strokes

After you paint a set of strokes and then click Finish, the strokes become a single Photo-Draw object. Any change you make to the object, such as changing the brush or color, affects all the strokes in the object.

TRY THIS

Apply effects to paint strokes. *Try applying a designer effect or even a designer 3-D effect to a set of paint strokes. PhotoDraw takes a long time to create the effects, but the result can be amazing.*

Modify a Paint Object

1. Click a paint object (a set of strokes).

2. Click Outline on the visual menu.

3. Click Artistic Brushes or Photo Brushes on the Outline menu.

4. Change options on the Outline workpane.

5. For further options, click Settings in the workpane list.

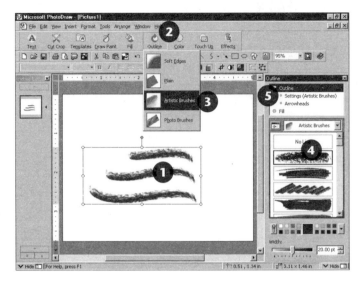

Softening the Edges of Objects

To give a shape or painted object a soft, gauzy look, you can soften its edges. Photo-Draw accomplishes this by making some of the pixels along the edges of the object semitransparent so the edges appear to fade.

Soften Edges

1. Click the object whose edges you want to soften.

2. Click Outline on the visual menu.

3. Click Soft Edges on the Outline menu.

4. Drag the Soft Edges slider on the workpane to change the softness of the object's edges.

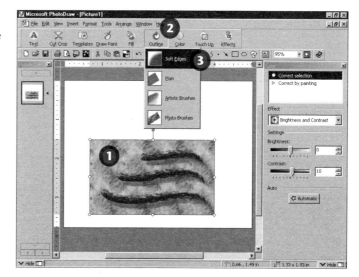

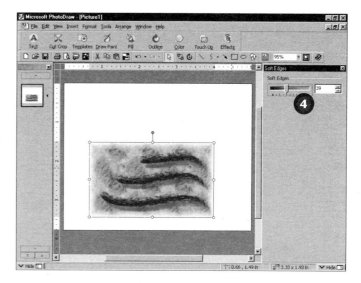

Reshaping Shapes

S imple shapes, such as lines, curves, rectangles, and ellipses, are made up of segments that connect points. Normally, you work with the overall shape, changing its outline and fill and resizing or repositioning it. But you can also switch to a special mode in Microsoft PhotoDraw that allows you to edit a shape's points one by one. In Edit Points mode, you can move points, add and delete points, and reshape the segments that connect points. These features allow you to finely adjust the shape of an object.

Entering and Exiting Edit Points Mode

Generally, you don't have to switch to special modes in PhotoDraw to get most tasks accomplished. But to reshape objects, you must enter Edit Points mode and stay in it until you are finished.

While in Edit Points mode, you can work with a shape's points and the segments that connect the points. When you exit Edit Points mode, you can once again make changes only to the overall shape.

TIP

Finding Edit Points. *You can find the Edit Points command only on the shortcut menu. It's not on the main menu or any of the toolbars.*

SEE ALSO

For information about changing the overall shape of an object, see Section 7, "Editing Individual Objects," on pages 65–84.

Enter and Exit Edit Points Mode

1. Click a shape with the right mouse button.

2. Click Edit Points on the shortcut menu.

3. To leave Edit Points mode, click Exit Edit Points on the small, floating Edit Points toolbar.

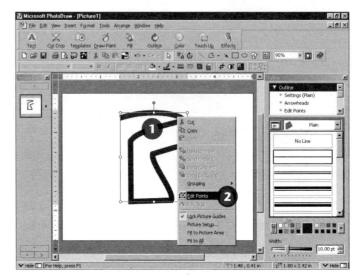

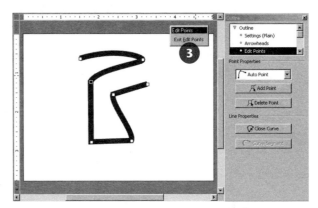

Moving a Point

When you enter Edit Points mode, you can see the points at the ends of the shape's segments. Because each point is at the vertex of two segments, moving a point changes the position of both segments.

Watch the mouse pointer.
The mouse pointer changes shape as you move it over objects. The shape of the mouse pointer reveals what actions are possible. For example, when you pass the mouse pointer over one of the object's points, it shows a four-way arrow to indicate that you can move the point.

Four-way
mouse pointer

Move a Point

1. Enter Edit Points mode.

2. Position the mouse pointer on the point to move.

3. Press and hold down the mouse button and drag the mouse pointer.

4. Continue editing the shape's points or exit Edit Points mode.

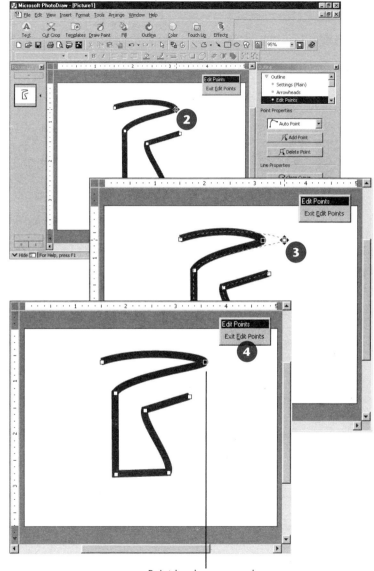

Point has been moved.

Adding and Deleting Points

Shapes have existing points at the ends of their segments, but to gain more control over the shape of a segment, you can add more points to create additional segments that you can move individually.

When you delete a point, the two segments that are connected by the point become a single segment.

TIP

The Add Point button. *You can also add points without reshaping a segment by clicking a segment between two points and then clicking the Add Point button on the workpane.*

Add a Point

1. Enter Edit Points mode.

2. Position the mouse pointer on a segment between two points.

3. Hold down the mouse button and drag the mouse pointer.

4. Continue editing the shape's points or exit Edit Points mode.

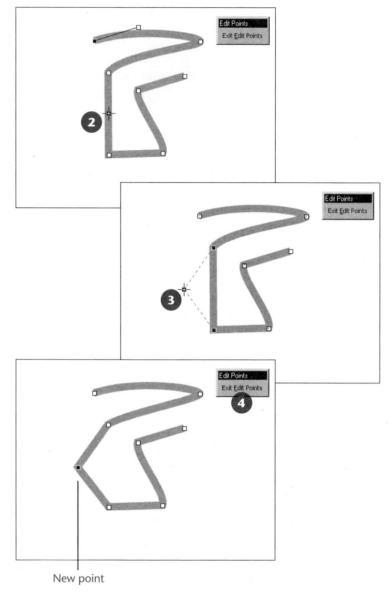

New point

Delete a Point

① Enter Edit Points mode.

② Press and hold down the Ctrl key on the keyboard.

③ Click a point.

④ Continue editing the shape's points or exit Edit Points mode.

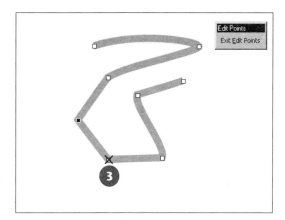

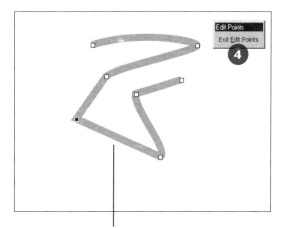

Point has been removed.

About Point Types

A point at the meeting place of two straight-line segments is an *auto point*. You can move an Auto Point to change the position of the two segments, but that's about it.

When a point joins two curved segments, things become much more interesting. As you'll learn on the opposite page, you can change the point to one of three other point types. These point types display a pair of handles, one for each curved segment at either side of the point. By dragging these handles, you can pull the bend of the curves to adjust how they approach and depart from the point.

When you drag a handle on a *symmetric point*, the handle on the other side of the point moves an equal distance in the opposite direction. This causes the curve to flow smoothly through the point.

The handles of a *smooth point* also move in opposite directions, but you can change their length separately so you can give the curve on one side of the point more of a bend.

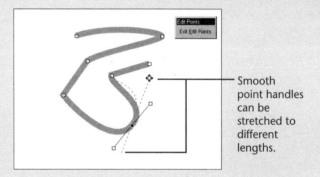

Smooth point handles can be stretched to different lengths.

You can move the handles of a *corner point* independently. The curve no longer flows smoothly through the point. Instead, it forms a sharp angle or corner.

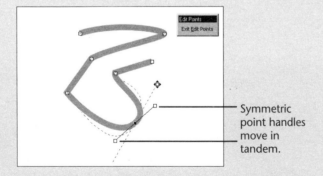

Symmetric point handles move in tandem.

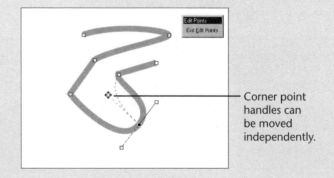

Corner point handles can be moved independently.

Changing the Point Type

When a point joins two curves, you can change it from the default auto point to one of three other point types that allow you to change how the curves pass through the point. The sidebar on the opposite page covers these alternate point types.

Change the Point Type

1. Enter Edit Points mode.

2. Click a point.

3. Click the drop-down arrow next to the Point Type box.

4. Click a point type in the Point Type list.

5. Drag one or both handles to reshape the curve as it passes through the point.

6. Continue editing the shape's points or exit Edit Points mode.

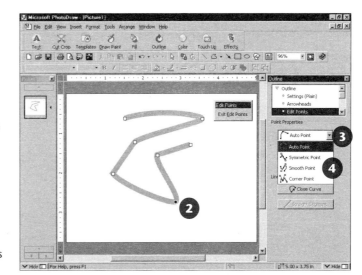

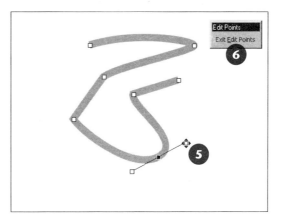

Curve or Straighten a Line Segment

A segment between two points is either a curve or a straight line depending on the shape of the object. The segments of a rectangle are all straight lines, for example, while the segments of an ellipse are curved. You can easily convert a segment from curved to straight or vice versa.

Curve or Straighten a Segment

1. Enter Edit Points mode.

2. Click a segment (between two points) on the shape.

3. Click the Curve Segment button on the workpane if the segment is straight or click the Straight Segment button on the workpane if the segment is curved.

4. Continue editing the shape's points or exit Edit Points mode.

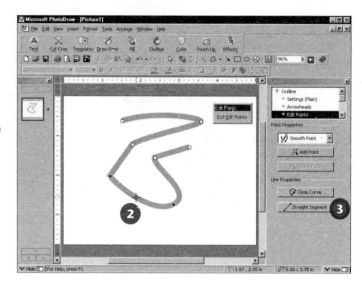

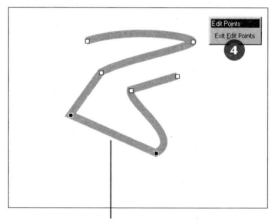

Curved segment is now straight.

Opening and Closing Curves

Closing a curve adds a straight segment between the first and last points of the curve. Opening a curve removes one of the segments.

Even when a curve is open, you can still change the fill as if the curve were a closed shape.

SEE ALSO

For more information about changing the fill of a curve, see "Drawing Curves" on page 157.

Open and Close a Curve

1. Enter Edit Points mode.

2. Click the Open Curve button on the workpane to open a closed curve or click the Close Curve button on the workpane to join the first and last points with a straight-line segment.

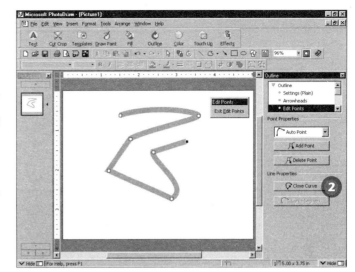

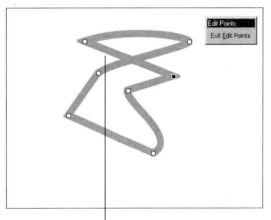

Added segment closes curve.

Saving, Sending, and Printing

Even after you've got the perfect picture in Microsoft PhotoDraw, you still need to save it, send it, or print it or else your masterpiece will revert to digital dust when you quit PhotoDraw.

Saving a PhotoDraw picture is no harder than saving a file in any program, but saving the right file format for use in other graphics, desktop publishing, or Web page design programs is more challenging. PhotoDraw's Save For Use In Wizard helps by stepping you through saving a file in the format that is best for your needs.

PhotoDraw makes e-mailing and printing pictures easy, too. The Send To Mail Recipient command deposits a picture in your outbox, and PhotoDraw's advanced printing capabilities let you print not only single pictures, but rows of them in a pattern preformatted to fit sheets of labels and cards that you can buy from your favorite stationery dealer.

Saving a Picture

To make any picture in the picture list available the next time you start PhotoDraw, you must save it in its own Photo-Draw file (a MIX file). If you do not save a picture in the picture list, it will be erased when you quit PhotoDraw.

A PhotoDraw MIX (.mix) file saves everything on both the scratch and picture areas in the picture. To save a picture for use on a Web site or in a Microsoft Office file, you should use the Save For Use In Wizard, described on pages 184–190.

pages 184–190.

TIP

Is the picture saved?
To check whether a picture is saved, click the picture in the picture list and then check the title bar at the top of the Photo-Draw window. If the picture is saved, the name you have given the file appears next to Microsoft PhotoDraw. *Otherwise, a generic name appears, such as Picture1, Picture2, or Picture3.*

Save a Picture

1 If the picture is not visible in the work area, click it in the picture list.

2 Click the Save button on the Standard toolbar.

3 Click a disk and folder in the Save In list.

4 Enter a name for the file.

5 Click Save.

Save button

Saving a Graphics File

To create a file that other graphics programs can read, you must save the picture area as a standard graphics file, such as a TIFF or JPEG file. Only the parts of objects that are within the rectangular picture area are saved. Everything outside the picture area, even the parts of objects in the picture area that fall outside of it, are cut off.

TIP

Why just the picture area?
Bitmaps, the type of graphics files that you can save in Photo-Draw and then open in other graphics programs and Web browsers, are always rectangular, and you print on rectangular paper. By setting the size of the picture area, you define the rectangular area that you want included in the bitmap or on the printed page.

Save As a Graphics File

1. If the picture is not visible in the work area, click it in the picture list.

2. Click the Save button on the Standard toolbar or, if you have already saved the picture as a MIX file, click Save As on the File menu.

3. Click a disk and folder in the Save In list.

4. Enter a name for the file.

5. Click the drop-down arrow next to the Save As Type box and click a file type in the list.

6. Click Save.

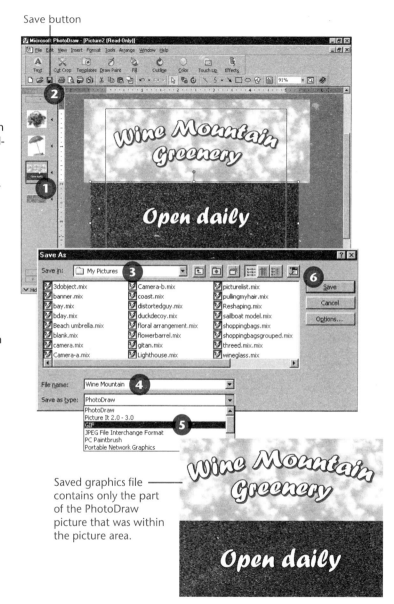

Save button

Saved graphics file contains only the part of the PhotoDraw picture that was within the picture area.

About Graphics Files

PhotoDraw's MIX file format is fine for a picture that you want to save and open again later to resume working just where you left off. MIX files contain only one picture in each file, though, so you can't save the entire picture list to create a snapshot of the all the pictures you're working with. Instead, you must save in its own MIX file each picture in the picture list. To save the MIX files together, you may want to put them all in the same folder on your hard disk.

MIX files are proprietary to PhotoDraw so they're not usable in other programs. If you want to use a picture in another program, such as a desktop publishing program or presentation graphics software, or if you plan to send a picture to someone in an e-mail message, you must choose a standard graphics file format in which to save the picture, such as GIF or JPEG. Your choice of file format depends on how you'll use the picture. Each file format offers a different tradeoff between picture fidelity and file compression. Picture fidelity preserves the quality of the original image. File compression produces a file that is small enough to store easily or transmit across the Internet by modem. Unfortunately, these two usually have an inverse relationship. Fidelity suffers as compression improves.

A file format that offers a good fidelity/compression tradeoff is just around the corner. PNG (.png) files are heavily compressed, but they still offer faithful representations of the original image without the loss in picture

The Save For Use In Wizard asks where you plan to put a picture to determine the best file format.

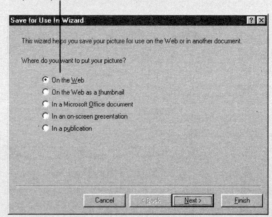

quality that usually appears during compression. The Microsoft Office 2000 programs and Internet Explorer 5 can read and display PNG files, but until all programs and Web browsers can read PNG files, you should probably use traditional graphics file formats that are universally accepted, such as TIFF (.tif), GIF (.gif), and JPEG (.jpg).

Choosing an appropriate file format usually requires that you understand the various graphics file formats and their comparative advantages. Fortunately, PhotoDraw's Save For Use In Wizard can help you choose the best file format for your pictures.

Web Picture File Types

All Web browsers can display two picture file types, GIF and JPEG. Microsoft Internet Explorer 5 and the Microsoft Office 2000 applications can also display PNG files, a new and improved file format for saving and displaying pictures. All three file formats for graphics compress pictures to make them small and easy to send over the Internet, but they use different compression methods, which have relative advantages and disadvantages.

GIF is probably the best file format to use when a picture consists primarily of text and line drawings. GIF files use moderate compression so they don't shrink files as much as JPEG, but they also don't cause the loss of clarity that you can see sometimes in JPEG files. As a result, the fine lines in text and drawings remain clear and distinct, while in JPEG files, they can become blotchy and broken. GIF files also have the capability to show transparent areas, unlike JPEGs. Because they can show transparency around a figure, they can display nonrectangular graphics on Web pages.

The primary disadvantage of GIF files is that they display only 256 colors, unlike JPEG files, which can show millions of colors. As a result, they're unsatisfactory for displaying photos that have fine gradations in color. To compensate, GIF files can *dither* colors, or put pixels of two colors adjacent to give the impression of a third color. But dithering in images can be seen easily sometimes, and it can make photos look like computer-synthesized pictures.

JPEG is the best file format to use for photographic images. Because JPEG files can display millions of colors, they don't dither. Moreover, the heavy compression in JPEG files produces remarkably small file sizes. A picture that is more than 1 MB in an uncompressed Windows BMP file can become less than 100 KB in a JPEG file.

The tradeoff for the high compression that JPEG files achieve is a loss in image quality. JPEG files compress images by analyzing the colors in small grids across a photo and substituting a single, average color in each grid. With less color information in the file, a JPEG file can be smaller. But averaging colors reduces the number of shades you see in subtle color transitions, such as the varying blues of the sky. If you zoom in closely, you see stripes of a few shades rather than a gradual transition through many shades. The compression in JPEGs also makes fine lines look blotchy. Small text characters, in particular, can become hard to read.

Another disadvantage of JPEG files is that they cannot display transparency. Transparent areas are converted to a solid color, so they always appear rectangular on Web pages.

PNG, a newly introduced file format for graphics, can display millions of colors and show transparency, so it's well suited for any type of picture, text, or drawing. Only the newest Web browsers and applications can display PNG files, though, so many people who view your Web page using older browsers may not see the PNG files you've used.

15

Saving a Picture for a Microsoft Office Document

All Microsoft Office 2000 applications can read and display PNG files, the newest and most full-featured file format for pictures. PNG files are described in the sidebar on page 183.

When you use the Save For Use In Wizard and choose to save a picture for use in a Microsoft Office document, the picture is saved in a PNG file. After you save a PNG file on your hard disk drive, you can open a document in an Office application and insert the PNG file.

Save for Use in a Microsoft Office Document

1. If the picture is not visible in the work area, click it in the picture list.

2. Click Save For Use In on the File menu.

3. Click In A Microsoft Office Document, and then click Next.

4. Review the information on the last screen of the wizard, and then click Save.

5. Click a disk drive and folder in the Save In list.

6. Enter a name for the file.

7. Click Save.

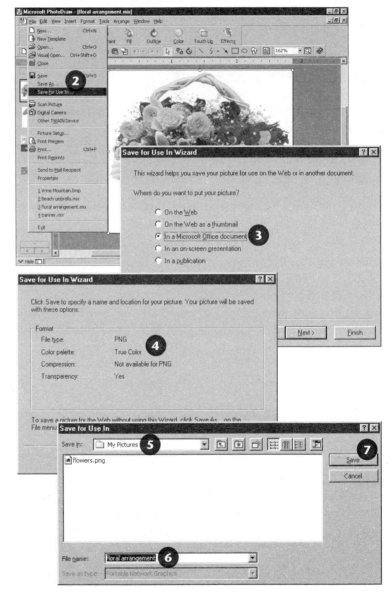

Saving a Photo for the Web

Even though PNG is an up-and-coming file format, the safe choice for saving a Web page photo that everyone can see is still GIF or JPEG. The Save For Use In Wizard, which helps you save an image in the best format for your needs, offers GIF and several compression levels of JPEG.

TIP

Making PNGs. *If you still want to save a picture in a PNG file, use the "Save As a Graphics File" procedure on page 181.*

TIP

Web picture quality. *To save the smallest possible file size, you should switch to Web picture quality before saving the file. Click Options on the Tools menu and then click Web on the Picture Quality tab of the Options dialog box.*

Save for Use on the Web

1. If the picture is not visible in the work area, click it in the picture list.

2. Click Save For Use In on the File menu.

3. Click On The Web and click Next.

4. Click a connection speed that you anticipate most viewers will use.

5. Scroll through and compare the quality and download times of the sample images. Click the sample that offers the best combination, and then click Next.

6. Review the information on the last screen of the wizard and click Save.

7. Click a disk and folder in the Save In list.

8. Enter a name for the file.

9. Click Save.

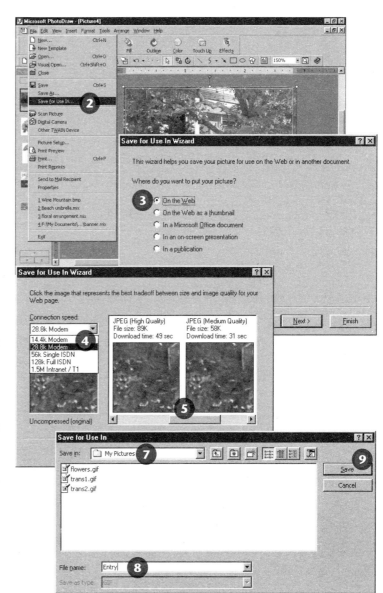

Saving a Picture with Transparency for the Web

If a picture you've created for the Web has areas of transparency, the Save For Use In Wizard recognizes the transparency and helps you determine how those areas will look. Transparent areas can let the background of the Web page show through, or they can show a solid color that complements the background of the Web page.

TIP

Interactive wizard. *The successive dialog boxes you see in the Save For Use In Wizard change depending on the choices you make at each step.*

Save for Use on the Web with Transparency

1. If the picture is not visible in the work area, click it in the picture list.

2. Click Save For Use In on the File menu, click On The Web on the first page of the Save For Use In Wizard, and click Next.

3. If you want the picture to appear in a solid-color rectangular area on the Web page, click Fill Them With the Background Color and click Next. Otherwise, just click Next.

4. If you chose to let the Web page background show through at step 3, do one of the following:

   ◆ Click My Web Page's Background Is The Following Solid Color, click a color on the color drop-down list, click Next, and skip to step 7.

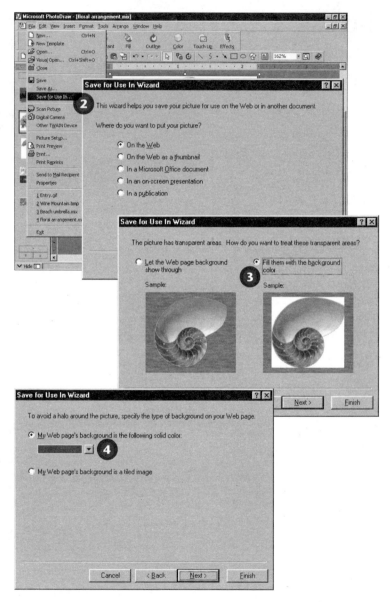

Avoiding a fringe. *If you choose to leave areas of transparency in a picture when you use the wizard, you are prompted to choose a color so PhotoDraw can mix pixels at the edge of the transparent areas with pixels of the background color. This helps blend the image into the background seamlessly. Without such blending, the transparent areas may be surrounded by an unattractive fringe of dark pixels on the Web page.*

◆ Or, if the Web page background is not a solid color, click My Web Page's Background Is A Tiled Image, click Next, and skip to step 7.

5 If you chose to fill the background with a solid color at step 3, click a color in the drop-down list and click Next.

6 Click a connection speed, scroll through the file types, click the best tradeoff between speed and image quality, and click Next.

7 Review the information on the last screen of the wizard and then click Save.

8 Click a disk and folder in the Save In list.

9 Enter a name for the file and click Save.

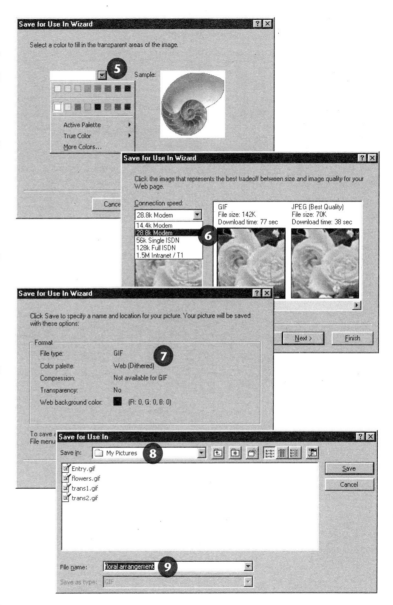

15

Saving a Picture As a Web Page Thumbnail

To speed up Web pages, designers often use small, thumbnail versions of pictures that viewers can click to open a full-size image. Photo-Draw can automatically save any picture as a small, 96-by-96-pixel square that will appear to be about one inch across on a Web page.

TIP

Adding a designer edge to a thumbnail. *After you save a picture as a thumbnail, you may want to open it, give it a designer edge to convert it from a flat square into a button, and then resave it.*

Save for Use As a Thumbnail

1. If the picture is not visible in the work area, click it in the picture list.

2. Save For Use In on the File menu.

3. Click On The Web As A Thumbnail, and then click Next.

4. Click a connection speed, scroll through and compare the quality and download times of the sample images, and click the sample that offers the best tradeoff. Click Next.

5. On the last screen of the wizard, click Save.

6. Click a disk and folder in the Save In list.

7. Enter a name for the file.

8. Click Save.

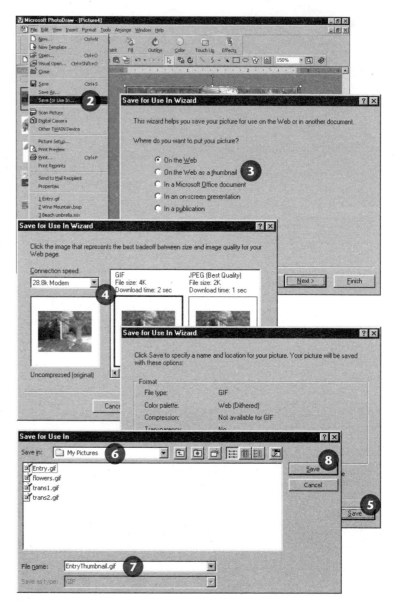

Saving a Picture for PowerPoint

Microsoft PowerPoint, the most popular presentation graphics program, produces on-screen slide shows for meetings and lectures. Power-Point slides can contain text, charts, and graphics that you create in PowerPoint. They can also display pictures produced by other programs, like PhotoDraw.

TIP

Earlier PowerPoint versions.
If you use PowerPoint 2000, you can follow the procedure on this page to save a file to insert onto a slide. If you use an earlier version of PowerPoint, you can save a picture as a standard graphics file, such as a JPEG or GIF file. You can then insert the file into a slide in PowerPoint.

Save for Use in an On-screen Presentation

1. If the picture is not visible in the work area, click it in the picture list.

2. Click File on the Menu bar and then click Save For Use In on the File menu.

3. Click In An On-screen Presentation, and then click Next.

4. On the last screen of the wizard, click Save.

5. Click a disk and folder in the Save In list.

6. Enter a name for the file.

7. Click Save.

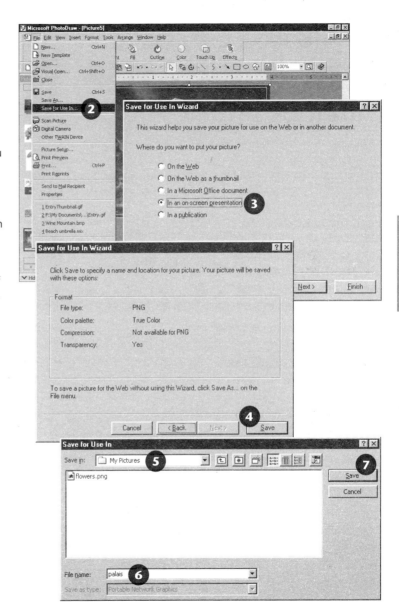

Saving a Picture for a Printed Publication

If you plan to use a picture in a printed document created with a desktop publishing program such as Microsoft Publisher or Adobe Page-Maker, you can use the Save For Use In Wizard to create a TIFF file. TIFF files are the most common graphics file format for printing and publishing.

TIP

Producing grayscale TIFFs.
If you know that you will be printing a publication on a laser printer, you can convert the picture to grayscale to see in advance how it will look on a black and white printer. For information about converting a picture to grayscale, see "Converting an Object to Grayscale" on page 92.

Save for Use in a Publication

1 If the picture is not visible in the work area, click it in the picture list.

2 Click Save For Use In on the File menu.

3 Click In A Publication, and then click Next.

4 Review the information on the last screen of the wizard, and then click Save.

5 Click a disk and folder in the Save In list.

6 Enter a name for the file.

7 Click Save.

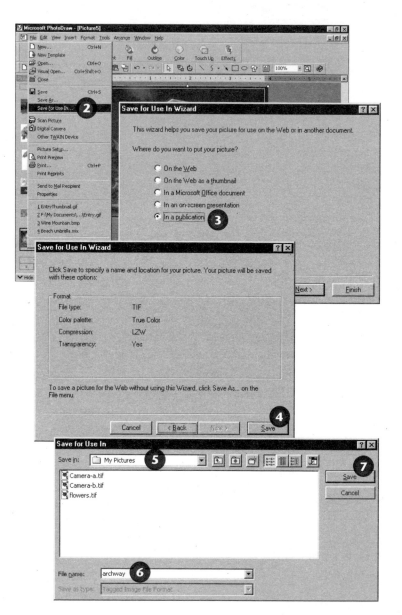

Sending a Picture by E-mail

To exchange a picture with someone else who also uses PhotoDraw, you can use the Send To Mail Recipient command. This creates a new mail message in your e-mail program and attaches a file containing a copy of the current picture. The file is in PhotoDraw format, so only another PhotoDraw user can view it.

If the e-mail recipient does not have PhotoDraw, you should save the picture as a GIF or JPEG file and then use your mail program to send the file as an attachment. The recipient can view the file using any Web browser.

Send to Mail Recipient

1. Click Send To Mail Recipient on the File menu.

2. Use the options in your e-mail program to address and send the message.

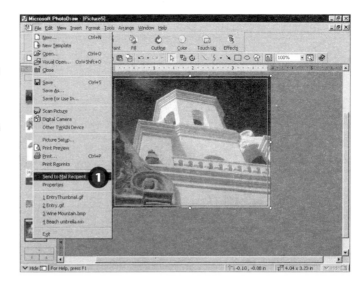

Printing Single Images

PhotoDraw can print a picture as is or automatically size it to standard photographic dimensions, such as 4 by 6 inches, 5 by 7 inches, or 15 by 20 centimeters. PhotoDraw also offers three standard choices of print quality (Good, Better, and Best) with corresponding print resolutions. The better the print quality, the longer most printers will take to print the image.

TIP

Print resolutions. *The highest resolution in the Print Quality list matches the best picture quality setting in PhotoDraw. Even if your printer is capable of printing at a higher resolution than that shown in the list, the image still will not print at any greater resolution than the best quality setting in PhotoDraw.*

Print

1. Click Print on the File menu.

2. Set the options on the General tab to change the number of copies to be printed, the print quality (Good, Better, Best), and the paper orientation (Portrait or Landscape).

3. Leave the Match Screen Colors check box selected to let PhotoDraw adjust the colors that will be printed so the printed page looks like the image on your monitor.

4. Click Print Crop Marks if you want small braces to print on the page to show the size of the picture area.

5. Check the preview on the General tab and click the Size tab if you want to change the size of the image on the page.

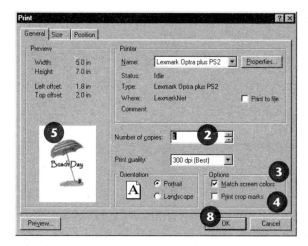

6. To change the size, click Fit To Page, choose one of the sizes from the Photographic Size list or click Custom Size and enter measurements in the Width and Height boxes.

7. To change the position of the image on the page, click the Position tab, clear the Center On Page check boxes, and change the Offset numbers to alter the margins.

8. Click the General tab again and click OK to begin printing.

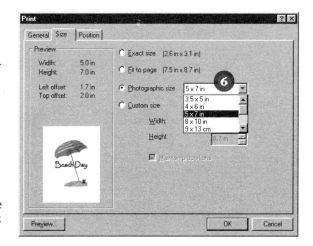

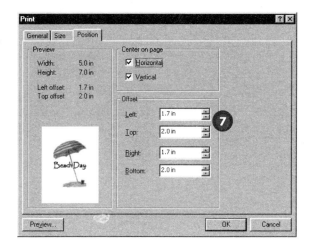

Printing Labels, Cards, and Photo Sheets

Reprints are sheets of images that you can print on labels, cards, and stickers that are designed to feed through a standard printer. PhotoDraw comes with built-in templates for dozens of commercially available products, such as computer labels.

You can also use Print Reprints to print photos on sheets that you can cut apart and then hand out.

Print Reprints

1. Open the picture or pictures that you want to print so it appears in the picture list.

2. Click Print Reprints on the File menu.

3. If the printer you want to use is not shown on the Reprints workpane, click the drop-down arrow next to the Destination Printer box and choose the printer you want from the list. Click Next.

4. Click a category in the Category list and click a template in the Template list. Click Next.

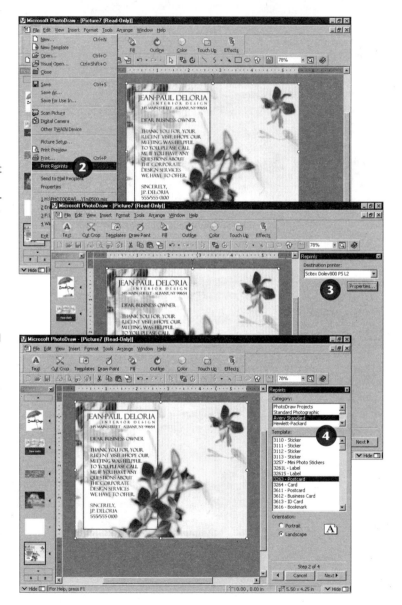

Choosing an insert method.
When you choose an insert method at step 6, PhotoDraw gives you the option to fit the object within the space available (without stretching it) or to fill the space, even if it means stretching the image out of shape. If you want the image to remain the same shape, choose Fit Within.

Saving the template for later printing. *You can save the template that you've created so you can print it again in the future.*

5 To print sheets of the same image, click One. To print multiple images, click Many.

6 Click an Insert Method on the reprints workpane.

7 Drag a picture from the picture list onto the template or, if you clicked Many at step 3, drag multiple images from the picture list into the grid of the template.

8 Click Finish to print the reprints.

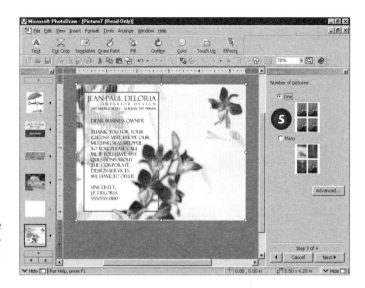

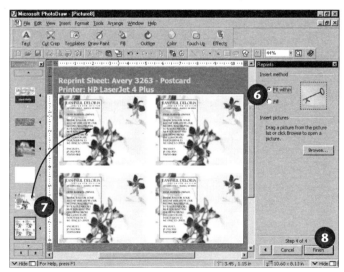

15

Project: Creating Buttons for a Web Page

This short, nine-step project demonstrates how you might use the tools that are truly unique to Microsoft PhotoDraw in a real-world scenario. In this example, your goal is to quickly create a matching set of buttons for a travel company's Web page.

To accomplish the project, you will use a template, the picture list, the object list, and the picture area in concert with several simple PhotoDraw commands to produce professional-looking Web page buttons.

Step 1. Setting Up for the Project

Because you will be creating elements for a Web page, you should set the picture quality for this project to Web, the setting that is appropriate for working on Web page graphics.

Choosing Web for the picture quality sets the resolution, or the number of pixels per inch, to a setting that is appropriate for Web page graphics, which are displayed at the resolution of typical monitor, or 96 pixels per inch.

TIP

Keeping files small. *For the Web, you want to create the best quality images in the smallest possible files. Setting the picture quality in PhotoDraw to Web saves graphics at 96 pixels per inch, the highest resolution at which a monitor can display Web pages. Using a higher picture quality setting only creates larger files that are displayed no better.*

Set Up for the Project

1. Click Options on the Tools menu.

2. Click the Picture Quality tab in the Options dialog box.

3. In the Picture Quality area, click Web.

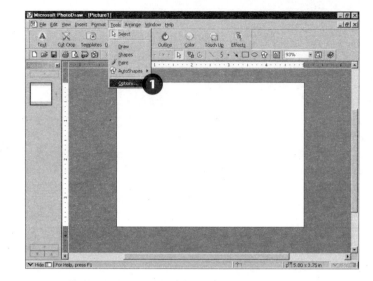

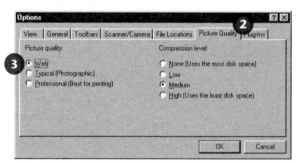

Step 2. Creating the Sample Web Page

To properly size the buttons, you can create a prototype Web page and place a sample button on it. The size of the prototype Web page should be approximately 600 pixels wide by 300 pixels high, the dimensions of the space visible within a typical browser window on a 640-by-480-pixel screen. A rectangle that is 600 by 300 pixels is approximately the size of the usable space left over after you subtract the space used by the browser's title bar, toolbars, and status bar.

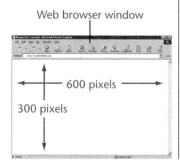

Web browser window

← 600 pixels →

300 pixels

Create a Sample Web Page

1 Click New on the File menu.

2 Click Picture Setup on the File menu.

3 Click the drop-down arrow next to the Units box and click Pixels in the Units list.

4 Enter 600 in the Width box and 300 in the Height box.

5 Click OK.

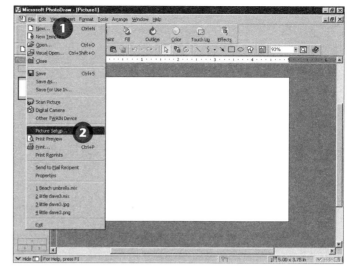

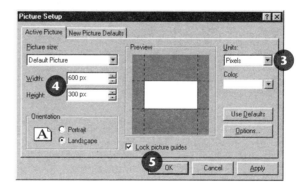

16

Step 3. Creating the First Button

For this travel-related project, you'll use an appropriate Web Graphics template to create a sample rectangular button. In your own projects, you can use any button template to achieve a different design.

In this procedure, you use a template to create the first button, which will be the basis for the other buttons that you will create in later steps.

SEE ALSO

For more information about using templates, see Section 12, "Creating Projects from Templates," on page 141.

Create a Button

1. Click Templates on the visual menu.

2. Click Web Graphics on the Templates menu.

3. Click Rectangular Buttons in the gallery.

4. Double-click the Map Rectangle style.

5. Keep clicking Next on the workpane until you reach the last step of the wizard, and then click Finish.

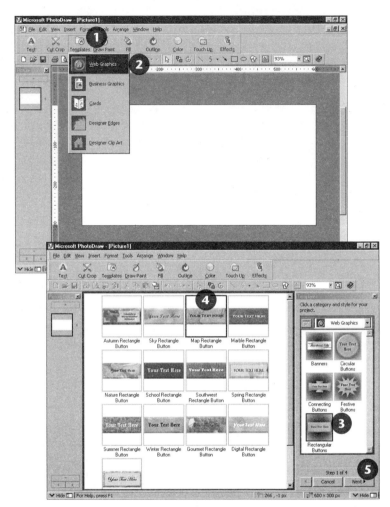

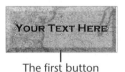

The first button

Step 4. Sizing the Button

In this step, you place the button on the prototype Web page to gauge its size in relation to the overall page area. The initial size of the button delivered by the template is too large for the page, so you reduce the button to a size that fits neatly on the side of the page.

To ensure that the button face and button text both shrink together, you group them into a single item. Reducing the group then reduces each component of the group proportionately.

Size the Button

1. Click the prototype Web page in the picture list.

2. Click the arrow button next to the button picture in the picture list.

3. Click All in the object list.

4. Drag an object from the object list onto the prototype Web page picture.

5. Close the object list.

6. Click Group on the Arrange menu.

7. Zoom in to the button and drag a handle to reduce the button to approximately 100 by 40 pixels, as indicated on the status bar.

8. Press F11 to zoom back out.

9. Drag the button onto the picture list to put it in its own picture, and close the Pan And Zoom dialog box to get it out of the way.

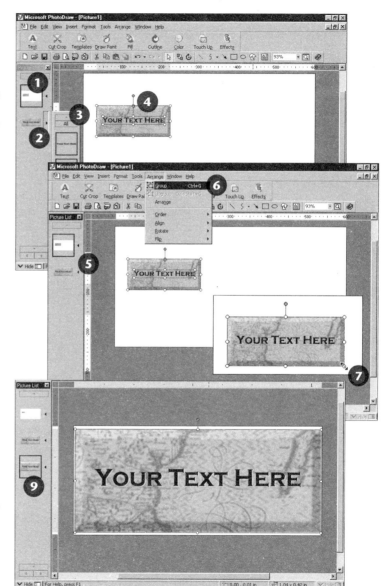

Step 5. Duplicating the Button

In this step, you duplicate the original button to create additional, identical buttons. In this example, you create three buttons that will have different text labels. In reality, you might want to make additional duplicates to produce even more buttons.

TIP

Keyboard shortcut. *To duplicate an object, you can also select it and press Ctrl+D on the keyboard.*

Duplicate the Button

1. Click the drop-down arrow next to the Zoom box and click 200% on the Zoom list.

2. Click Duplicate on the Edit menu.

3. Drag the duplicate above the original button.

4. Again click Duplicate on the Edit menu.

5. Drag the duplicate below the original button.

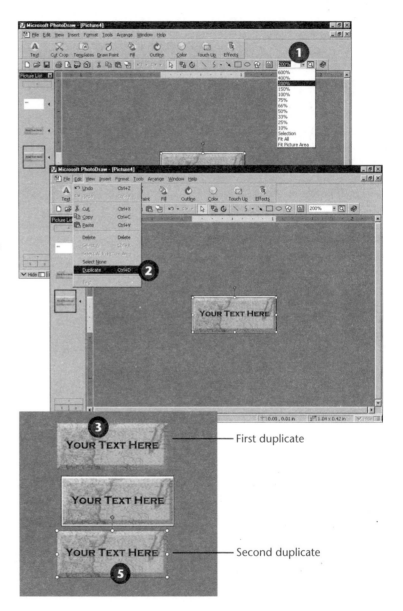

First duplicate

Second duplicate

Step 6. Editing the Button Text

To make each button unique, you must edit the text that appears on the button face. Because you grouped the buttons earlier to make sure that the button face and text shrunk proportionately, you must ungroup them before you can edit the text.

TIP

Enhancing the text. *In this short example, you use the text typeface provided by the template. When you create your own buttons, you can enhance the text by changing the typeface and adding effects, such as a shadow to make the text look raised.*

SEE ALSO

For more information about grouping and ungrouping objects, see "Grouping Objects" on page 137.

Edit the Button Text

1. Click the top button.

2. Click Ungroup on the Arrange menu.

3. Double-click the button text object.

4. Type **Products**.

5. For each of the other two buttons, select the button, click Ungroup on the Arrange menu, double-click the button text object, and enter replacement text. Type **Services** on one button and **Info** on the other.

6. Close the Text workpane to get it out of the way.

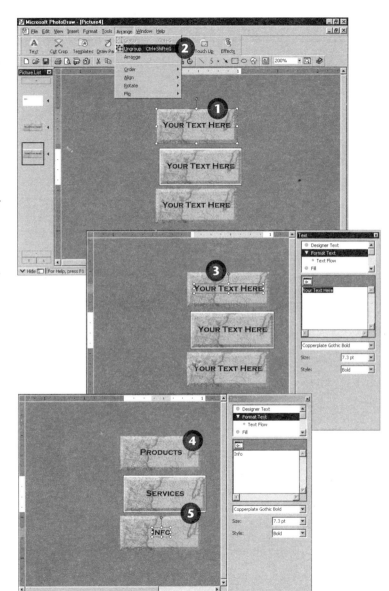

16

Step 7. Regrouping the Buttons

Although you don't have to regroup the buttons after you've edited their text, grouping them makes them easier to handle. The object list shows only three objects rather than six.

TIP

Saving objects flattens them. *When you save the contents of the picture area in a graphics file, such as a GIF or JPEG file, PhotoDraw informs you that it will flatten the objects. Although this sounds menacing, it simply means that the objects will be inseparable in the graphics file. If you also want a version whose objects are individually editable, you should save the picture as a standard PhotoDraw MIX file, too.*

SEE ALSO

For more information about saving pictures as graphics files, see "Saving a Graphics File" on page 181.

Regroup the Buttons

1. Click the text object on the top button.

2. Press and hold the Shift key and click the button face.

3. Click Group on the Arrange menu.

4. Repeat steps 1 through 3 above for the other two buttons.

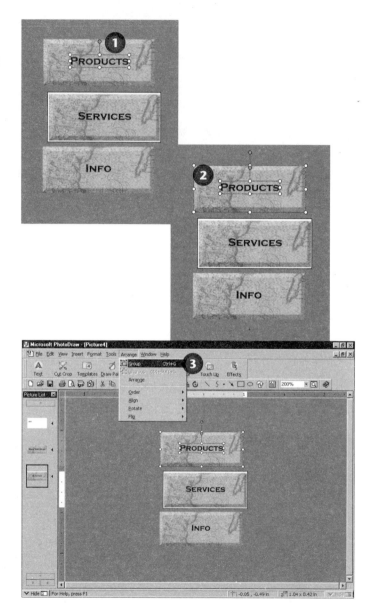

Step 8. Testing the Buttons

In this optional step, you arrange the buttons you've created on the prototype Web page as they will appear on the real Web page that you will assemble in a Web page design program, such as Microsoft FrontPage. This gives you the opportunity to see how they will fit so you can adjust them, if necessary, while you are still working with them in PhotoDraw.

Test the Buttons

1. Click the sample Web page picture in the picture list.

2. Press the Delete key to delete the original button.

3. Click the arrow button next to the third picture in the picture list to open its object list.

4. Drag each object (button) from the picture list onto the sample Web page picture.

5. Drag the buttons into position to see how they look or select them and use the Align options on the Arrange menu to line them up perfectly.

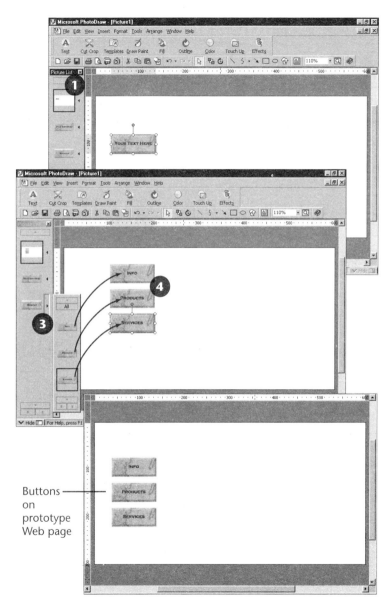

Buttons on prototype Web page

16

Step 9. Saving Each Button in a GIF File

In this step, you use the picture area to select and save each button in its own graphics file. Remember that only what is within the picture area is saved in the file. By fitting the picture area to each button and then saving the picture area to a file, you can put each button in a separate graphics file.

> **TIP**
>
> **Saving everything.** *To save everything in the picture, including the items that are outside the picture area (on the scratch area), you must save the picture in a PhotoDraw MIX file. The MIX file would contain all three buttons, regardless of the position of the picture area.*

Save the Buttons

1. Click the third picture in the picture list, which contains the three buttons.

2. Click the top button.

3. Click Fit Picture Area To Selection on the View menu.

4. Click Save As on the File menu.

5. Enter a name for the button.

6. Click the drop-down arrow next to the Save As Type box.

7. Click GIF in the Save As Type list.

8. Click Save.

9. Repeat steps 2 through 8, giving each button file a different name.

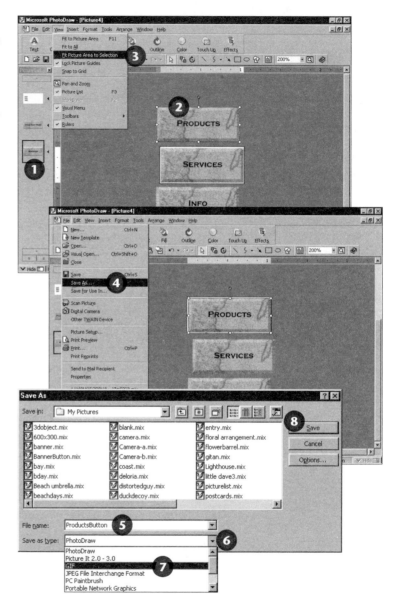

Getting Help

Microsoft PhotoDraw's Help window offers comprehensive, step-by-step help for all the tasks you can accomplish in the program. You can browse through a listing of help topics, or search for help topics by entering keywords. You can even type in real questions in plain language, such as *How do I change the color of an object?* PhotoDraw interprets the question and displays a list of possible answers.

Microsoft also maintains a Web site for PhotoDraw assistance, which offers common questions and answers, downloadable updates for the software, and additional templates that you can add to your collection.

Asking "What's This?"

To investigate any menu command, toolbar button, screen item, or workpane option, you can click What's This? on the Help menu and then click the command, button, item, or option. PhotoDraw opens a small ScreenTip box that describes the item you've clicked.

TIP

Help in dialog boxes. *For information about the commands in PhotoDraw dialog boxes, click the Help button (the question mark button) next to the Close button at the upper-right corner of the dialog box.*

Help

Ask "What's This?"

1. Click What's This? on the Help menu or press Shift+F1.

2. Click a menu command, toolbar button, screen item, or workpane option to see a description in a ScreenTip.

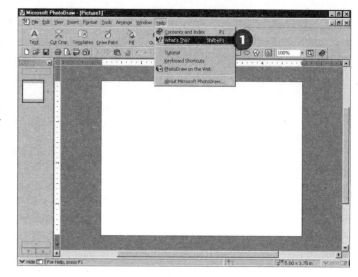

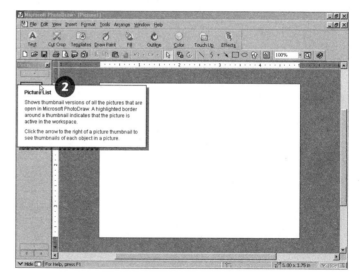

Opening the Help Window

Help topics for PhotoDraw are presented in the Help window, which has two side-by-side panes. The left pane displays three tabs (Contents, Answer Wizard, and Index) on which you can look up specific help topics. The right pane displays the topic you find.

TIP

Hiding the left pane. *To make the Help window smaller so you can leave it open next to the PhotoDraw window and refer to its instructions for a procedure, you can hide the left pane by clicking the Hide button on the toolbar.*

Hide

Open the Help Window

1. Click Contents And Index on the Help menu or press F1.

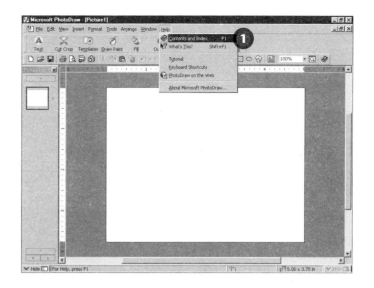

Help window

17

Browsing the Contents List

On the Contents tab in the left pane of the Help window, PhotoDraw displays a list of books. Each book contains a set of related topics. When you double-click a book, you can reveal its topics and then click a topic to open its text in the right pane.

TIP

Books within books. *When you double-click a book to reveal its topics and find more books listed among the topics, you can double-click these books to reveal sets of related subtopics.*

Browse the Contents List

1. Click Contents And Index on the Help menu or press the F1 key.

2. Double-click a book in the contents list in the left pane of the Help window to reveal its topics.

3. Click a topic to see its text in the right pane of the Help window.

4. Click underlined text in the right pane to jump to a related topic.

5. Double-click a book in the contents list again to hide its topics.

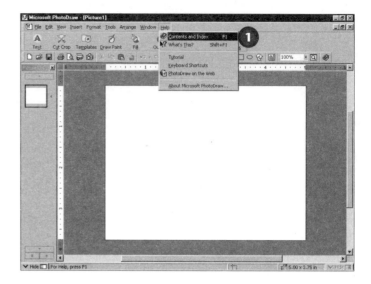

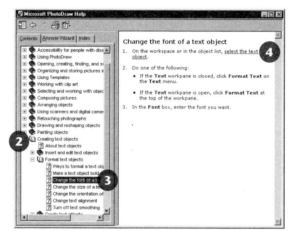

Asking the Answer Wizard

The Answer Wizard can find and display topics that answer questions you type. You can enter a question such as *How do I cut out part of a photo?* You don't have to enter it in any particular style. Just type a question as though you were asking a PhotoDraw expert.

Ask the Answer Wizard

1. Click Contents And Index on the Help menu or press the F1 key.

2. Click the Answer Wizard tab in the left pane of the Help window.

3. Type any question, such as *How do I add a shadow to an object?*

4. Click Search.

5. If more than one topic appears in the topic list in the left pane, click the topic that seems most appropriate and view the topic text in the right pane.

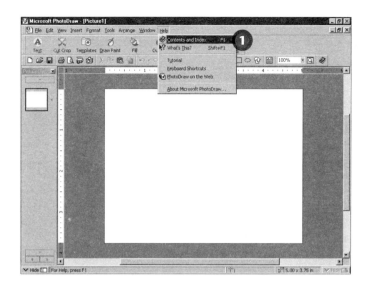

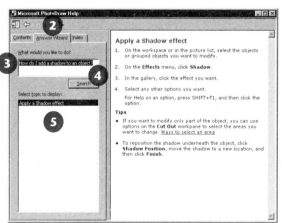

Finding Topics

To research information about a topic, you can enter a keyword in the Help index. PhotoDraw displays a list of topics that are related to the keyword.

TIP

Scrolling through the keyword list. *If you do not know the keyword that would be best to enter, you can scroll through the list of keywords shown in the Or Choose Keywords box on the Index tab. When you find an appropriate keyword, double-click it.*

Search for a Topic

1 Click Contents And Index on the Help menu or press the F1 key.

2 Click the Index tab in the left pane of the Help window.

3 Type a keyword such as *shadow* in the Type Keywords box.

4 Click Search.

5 Double-click a topic in the Choose A Topic list.

6 Read the topic text in the right pane of the Help window.

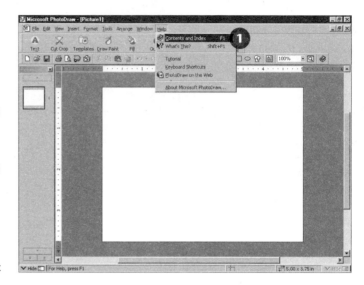

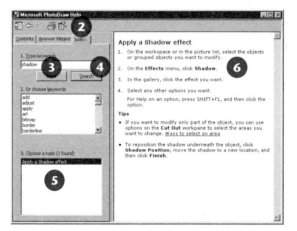

Printing Help Topics

If you'd prefer to have a printed page to refer to rather than read instructions from an online window, you can print any help topic text or set of related topics. To print a single topic, click the topic in the contents list and click the Print button. To print a set of topics, click the book in the contents list and click the Print button. In the Print Topics dialog box you can choose whether you want a single topic or the set of topics printed.

Print a Topic

1. Click Contents And Index on the Help menu or press the F1 key.

2. Use the contents list, the Answer Wizard, or the index to find a helpful topic.

3. Click the Print button on the toolbar in the Help window.

4. To print a single topic, click Print The Selected Topic. To print all the topics in the selected book, click Print The Selected Heading And All Subtopics.

5. Click OK.

Print button

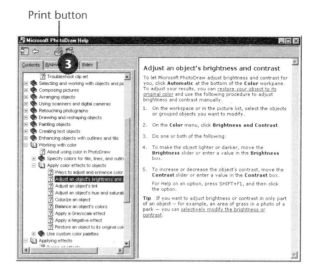

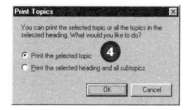

Using the Microsoft PhotoDraw Web Site

In addition to the help in the Help window, you can obtain help from a Microsoft Web site that is dedicated to Photo-Draw. At the PhotoDraw Web site, you can find questions and answers about Photo-Draw, downloadable updates to the program, additional templates that you can down-load, Microsoft Knowledge Base articles about Photo-Draw, a link to Microsoft Technical Support, and additional resources.

TIP

Web page changes. *Because the PhotoDraw Web site can be updated at any time, the Web pages you see may look different from the pages shown here.*

Access the Web Site for PhotoDraw

1. If your computer is not set to connect to the Internet auto-matically, establish a connection to the Internet with your modem.

2. Click PhotoDraw On The Web on the Help menu.

3. On the PhotoDraw Assistance Web page on the Microsoft Web site, click an underlined link for assistance or infor-mation.

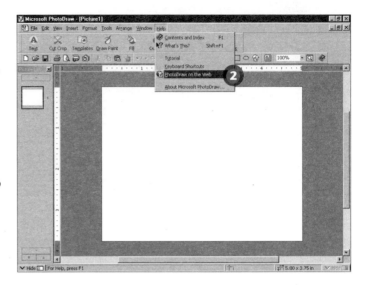

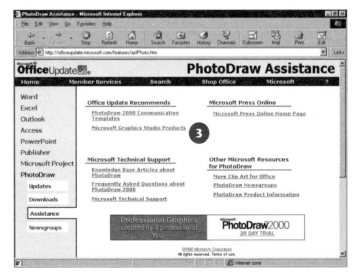

Visiting the PhotoDraw newsgroups. *In addition to the information on the Photo-Draw Assistance Web site, you can visit the PhotoDraw newsgroups on the Microsoft news server to participate in online discussions about using Photo-Draw. Click PhotoDraw Newsgroups on the PhotoDraw Assistance Web page. You can use any popular Internet newsreader software to access these discussions.*

The author's PhotoDraw-related Web pages. *For more information about this book and PhotoDraw, visit the author's Web site at www.studioserv.com.*

Download Updates

1. If your computer is not set to connect to the Internet automatically, establish a connection to the Internet with your modem.

2. Click PhotoDraw On The Web on the Help menu.

3. On the PhotoDraw Assistance Web page on the Microsoft Web site, click Updates.

4. Follow the instructions on the Updates page to install the update you want.

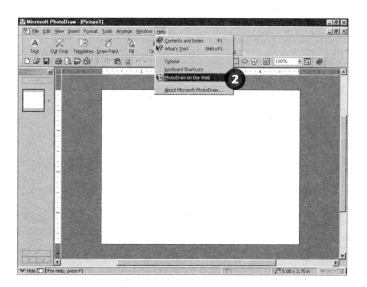

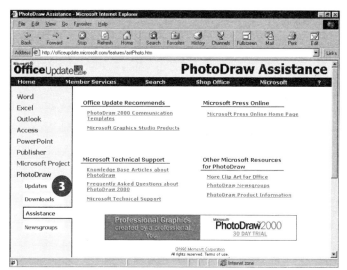

Downloading New Templates

You can download additional templates from the Photo-Draw Web site. These are free supplements to the hundreds of templates provided with the software. Additional templates are added from time to time, so be sure to check the site frequently for updates.

SEE ALSO

For information about using templates in PhotoDraw, see Section 12, "Creating Pictures from Templates," on page 141.

Download Templates

1. If your computer is not set to connect to the Internet automatically, establish a connection to the Internet.

2. Click PhotoDraw On The Web on the Help menu.

3. On the PhotoDraw Assistance Web page on the Microsoft Web site, click Downloads.

4. Follow the instructions on the Downloads page to select and install the additional templates that are available.

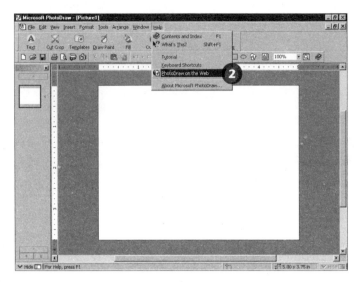

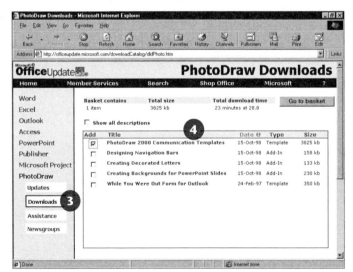

Index

Stephen W. Sagman is the New York–based author of more than 20 books on the subjects of graphics, Microsoft Windows, business applications, and online communications, and he has contributed to several more. For Microsoft Press, he has also written *Running PowerPoint*, now in its fourth edition, and *The Official Microsoft Image Composer Book*. His books have sold well over a million copies worldwide, and they have been translated into Chinese, Dutch, German, Greek, Hebrew, Japanese, Portuguese, Russian, Spanish, and Thai. His book *Traveling The Microsoft Network*, also published by Microsoft Press, was the recipient of the Award of Excellence from the Society for Technical Communication.

When he's not writing books, Steve runs Studioserv (www.studioserv.com), a technical communications company that offers book editing and production, user documentation, software training, and user interface design.

And when he's not writing or running his business, Steve plays jazz piano, sails his boat *Offline*, and toils in the fertile loam of his garden. He can be reached by e-mail at steves@studioserv.com.

The manuscript for this book was prepared and submitted to Microsoft Press in electronic form. Text files were prepared using Microsoft Word. Pages were composed in Adobe PageMaker for Windows by Studioserv (www.studioserv.com), with text in Stone Serif and display type in Stone Sans. Composed pages were delivered to the printer as electronic prepress files.

Cover Design
Tim Girvin Design

Principal Compositor
Sharon Bell,
Presentation Desktop
Publications

Indexer
Audrey Marr

Powerful
Web design tools
made easy.

U.S.A. **$24.99**
U.K. £22.99
Canada $35.99
ISBN 1-57231-836-8

WEB ADVERTISING AND MARKETING BY DESIGN provides hands-on, step-by-step instruction to help create dynamic advertising and promotional projects for the World Wide Web—whether or not you're an advertising or marketing professional. The book presents more than a dozen sample projects that you can customize and use, tapping powerful features from the latest Microsoft® Web design and content creation tools, including FrontPage®, Image Composer, GIF Animator, Microsoft Internet Explorer, and Microsoft Word. Each chapter discusses a project's theme and goals along with its size and scope, and then highlights key steps to help get your project organized and under way. Every project presents carefully constructed examples and precise information on creating effective graphic and text-based content.

Microsoft®_Press_

Be the master of your domain.

U.S.A. **$29.99**
U.K.   £27.99 [V.A.T. included]
Canada $42.99
ISBN 1-57231-922-4

The Webheads who build today's most-trafficked sites use advanced techniques such as server-side and browser-side scripting, Cascading Style Sheets, and Dynamic HTML to pull in the crowds. If you're ready to sprint past bland HTML, STUPID WEB TRICKS is the book you need. You'll get practical, clearly explained examples you can use as the basis for your own Web pages without being a programming guru.

Microsoft Press

Register Today!

Return this
Microsoft® PhotoDraw™ 2000 At a Glance
registration card today

Microsoft Press
mspress.microsoft.com

OWNER REGISTRATION CARD   **1-57231-954-2**

Microsoft® PhotoDraw™ 2000 At a Glance

_____ _____ _____
FIRST NAME   MIDDLE INITIAL   LAST NAME

_____
INSTITUTION OR COMPANY NAME

_____
ADDRESS

_____

_____ _____ _____
CITY   STATE   ZIP
                                                                           (   )
_____ _____
E-MAIL ADDRESS   PHONE NUMBER

U.S. and Canada addresses only. Fill in information above and mail postage-free.
Please mail only the bottom half of this page.

For information about Microsoft Press®

products, visit our Web site at

mspress.microsoft.com

Microsoft®*Press*